Write Your Book in a Day:

The Two Sisters Blueprint for Turning Your Book Dreams into Published Reality

Elizabeth Ann Atkins

&

Catherine M. Greenspan

TWO SISTERS ®
WRITING & PUBLISHING

Copyright Page
Copyrighted Material

Write Your Book in a Day:
The Two Sisters Blueprint for Turning Your Book Dreams into
Published Reality

For information about this title or to order other books and/or electronic media, contact the publisher:

Two Sisters Writing & Publishing®
TwoSistersWriting.com
18530 Mack Avenue, Suite 166
Grosse Pointe Farms, MI 48236

ISBN (Paperback) 978-1-970476-00-2
ISBN (eBook) 978-1-970476-01-9

Printed in the United States of America

No part of this manuscript is fiction. Some names of people and places have been changed.

Book cover art and design: Two Sisters Writing & Publishing®
Formatting: Illumination Graphics

TWO SISTERS
WRITING & PUBLISHING ®

Established 2016

*This book is our gift to you as we celebrate
our ten-year anniversary.*

DISCLAIMER

This book provides tools, structure, and guidance for the writing process. However, **results are never guaranteed**. Your success as an author depends on your personal effort, consistency, and follow-through. The authors and publisher make no promise that every reader will write, finish, publish, or profit from a book.

DEDICATION

We are dedicating this book to our parents because they instilled in us a passion for reading, writing, grammar, and storytelling, along with the solid values of discipline, integrity, commitment, perseverance, and purpose to commit our time and talent to elevating the greater good of our world.

We have immeasurable gratitude to our father, Thomas Lee Atkins, for demonstrating the power of writing and storytelling by journaling in steno notebooks every evening at the dining room table. We are also grateful that he encouraged our curiosity and love of nature, required us to speak the Queen's English, and taught us that love is the meaning of life.

We also have immeasurable gratitude to our mother, Judge Marylin E. Atkins, for showing us that very hard work pays off in beautiful ways, and that "sacrifice" in the moment is actually the best investment in an enriching and fulfilling future for yourself, your family, and the lives you touch. And we're thankful that she showed you can have fun while doing all of the above.

We are also very thankful that during the turbulent 1960s, our parents followed their hearts in the face of condemnation, all in the name of love and family, teaching us to blaze our own trails as unique and empowered girls and women.

Now, as we celebrate the ten-year anniversary of Two Sisters Writing & Publishing® with the release of this book, we present it to you in tribute to our parents who helped inspire this mission to showcase diverse voices, including our own, whose stories can uplift and inspire people everywhere.

We are living our dreams as change-makers, and with this book our intention is to help you write the change you wish to see in yourself and in the world.

ACKNOWLEDGMENTS

Teamwork makes the dream work!
And what we do is definitely a team sport.
So, we're sending big bursts of gratitude to all the amazing
people who've helped us reach our ten-year anniversary.
We especially want to thank:

* Our superstar authors—for entrusting us to write and publish your books. *Please see the list of our authors on page 211.*

* Our book coaching clients—for the honor of guiding your book-writing journey.

* Our graphic designers—Darlene and Dan Swanson of Van-garde Imagery, Inc.—for your professionalism, reliability, and commitment to excellence.

* Our graphic designer—Deborah Perdue of Illumination Graphics—for working your Merlin Magic so that every project sparkles.

* Our phenomenal project manager—Jessica Bonosoro—for your dependability and impeccable organizational skills, and your unwavering commitment to ensuring that every detail is handled with care and excellence.

* Our amazing editorial assistants—Reema Baydoun, Mahmuda Ahmed, Saara Kamal, Hazel Beauchamp, Emily Yarmak, Natalie Luterman, Annika Nori—for your eagle eyes, editorial expertise, cultural sensitivities,

and dependable excellence that helps polish every Two Sisters Writing & Publishing book to perfection.

※ Our website and brand manager—Sean Smith, founder of Ikusa—for helping us elevate our voice, expand our reach, and bring the Two Sisters brand to life with greater clarity, impact, and authority.

※ Our trademark attorney—Leah Halpert of Halpert Trademark Law—for applying your diligence, expertise, and thoughtful counsel to protect the Two Sisters brand and give us peace of mind by knowing that our vision, voice, and intellectual property are securely safeguarded.

※ Our publishing platform leaders—the phenomenal Paige Allen, Director of IngramSpark (Global) at Ingram Content Group; Key Account Sales Manager Leigh Pierce; and the extremely helpful and kind staff at IngramSpark.

※ Our family, friends, and fans who have cheered us on, purchased our books, and helped spread the word about all that we do.

※ Our dear friend and colleague Stephanie Steinberg, founder of The Detroit Writing Room and The New York Writing Room, for our many wonderful collaborations that help aspiring writers get the guidance they need to write and publish books.

✳ Our short story contest writers, including those who were published in our international anthologies in 2018 and 2019.

✳ Our media friends who have shined their spotlights on us, our books, and our authors during interviews for television, radio, newspapers, magazines, podcasts, and websites to share our uplifting messages with people everywhere.

✳ Our friends and colleagues who continue to refer amazing future authors to us so that we can help their publishing dreams come true.

CONTENTS

INTRODUCTION

You've been hearing the call within to write your book. Maybe you've silenced it for years, feeling too busy, overwhelmed, or afraid to answer.

The result? The quiet misery of an unwritten book that keeps tugging at your heart.

Don't worry, you're not alone. This is very common.

That's why we're thrilled to provide this book as your solution.

Inside, you'll learn the same mindset shifts, structuring tools, industry insights, and guidance that we use in our Write Your Book in a Day workshops, coaching courses, and retreats that create bestselling authors.

Whether you're writing a memoir, a how-to guide, a leadership book, a personal growth book, a novel, a family history, or your message to change the world, this book is your blueprint.

It helps you go from stuck and stalled to writing with speed and clarity. It wrenches you out of despair, procrastination, and writer's block, into courage and confidence where you're free to write from your heart and soul with your most authentic, bold voice. That's how you compose a unique and powerful book. This guide also demystifies the publishing process and helps you decide the best route for you. You'll also learn how to promote your book and prosper from it.

We created this book after witnessing—over and over again—that people have powerful stories, but they waste years not telling them.

They wait for the "perfect moment."

But they don't take action, and time keeps whizzing by with relentless speed. Meanwhile, their ideas—their life lessons and their legacies—sit unwritten.

Sometimes they get dementia and become unable to write a book. Others take their stories and wisdom to the grave.

That's tragic.

Because when you don't tell your story, the people who need to read it never get to be inspired, informed, entertained or even saved by you. Know this: your book isn't just about *you*. It's about all the people in the world who *need* it. So with this book, please take action now. Answer that call inside your heart.

Here's another benefit. Creating a physical book from an idea in your mind, and watching people delight in reading, learning, laughing, crying, and even transforming as a result, is an extraordinarily thrilling experience for *you*. Your book can empower you, prosper you, and elevate you as a thought leader, expert, and paid speaker. It can boost your business, bolster your branding, and attract new customers who are impressed that you literally "wrote the book" on your area of expertise. You could ascend to the status of a bestselling author and even get a lucrative movie deal.

The possibilities are limitless, and we want *you* to use this blueprint to bring your book-writing dreams into physical reality as a published author.

We're honored to serve as your guide, because the blueprint that we're sharing really works. We here at **Two Sisters Writing & Publishing®** have used it to write, edit, publish, and promote nearly seventy books, with seven more in varying stages of writing and publishing.

Now you're about to learn everything you need to know to write, publish, promote, and prosper with your book, including:

- How to shift your mindset from overwhelm and confusion to courage and confidence.

- How to focus your topic.

- How to outline your book.

- How to write suspenseful scenes.

- How to use writing techniques that engage your readers.

- How to get help to write your book.

- The five major ways to publish your book.

- How to promote your book.

- A strategy to launch onto the bestseller lists.

- How to make money as a published author.

- How to **start** and **finish.**

Your book is not a far-off fantasy.

It's close enough to touch.

As you move through our blueprint—step by step—you'll feel your confidence surging . . . the ideas flowing . . . and the chapters getting written.

You'll feel yourself becoming a published author.

So get ready to write.

Open your heart.

We're about to help make your dream real—in a single, life-changing day.

Let's do this! We wish you happy writing . . .

Elizabeth Ann Atkins & Catherine M. Greenspan
Co-Founders
Two Sisters Writing & Publishing®

HOW TO USE THIS BOOK

This book promises to help you *Write Your Book in a Day.* That means you will learn in one day's time everything you need to know to write, publish, and promote your memoir, business book, self-help book, novel, poetry collection, or other type of book.

It's best to schedule an entire day that you can devote to this experience. First, get a solid night's sleep so you're energized and focused. Also, prepare your workspace and stock it with writing supplies. Have brain-fueling snacks, beverages, and lunch available. Let everyone know that you're on a solo writing retreat, from morning until early evening, and that they should not disturb you. Turn off your devices, along with notifications on your phone, laptop, desktop, or tablet.

And now, let's get to work!

SECTION 1

GET CONFIDENCE, COURAGE & CLARITY

It's time for a mindset shift that makes you *obsessed* with writing, publishing, and promoting your book. So, let's rise above any fear, confusion, and procrastination to focus on the big picture vision for your book. We'll craft your Summary Sentence, which will serve as your North Star on your book-writing journey. Get ready to unleash your creativity to craft a bold, brave strategy to bring your book into the world.

FIND YOUR CONFIDENCE & COURAGE

Mindset Shifts for Writing Success

It's Time to Dream Big & Bold!
The key to success when you embark on your book-writing journey is to envision your destination—the "wildest dream" version of it!

Harriet Tubman, who risked her life many times to save others on unimaginable trips through life-threatening danger, said:

"Every great dream begins with a dreamer. Always remember, you have within you the strength, the patience, and the passion to reach for the stars to change the world."

She dreamed it. She did it. And she helped change the world.

Now's your time.

So, let's dream bigger than ever . . . and reach for the stars!

If it were that easy, you would have already done it. That's why we're presenting this book to help you navigate from wherever you're starting, to turning your book-writing dreams into published reality.

**Blast Past Writer's Block & Book Obstacles
with Your Five W's & H**
Something has stopped you from writing your book. And until you identify what's been holding you back and leaving you in the misery of an unwritten book and unfulfilled dream, you will never write and publish your memoir, novel, business book, or poetry collection.

Fear is probably part of the problem. Writing a book can be terrifying, because you're exposing your heart, soul, and most private thoughts to the entire world, forever. That's why self-doubt, fear, and anxiety can be vicious saboteurs.

Your mind floods with a deluge of questions, sinking your dream of becoming a published author, as waves of despair push you into procrastination, creative paralysis, and writer's block.

Will my book be good enough? What if nobody reads it? Or worse, what if people hate it? Or will they get mad at me? My parents/partner/relatives will be so disappointed and embarrassed if I share what I really think—and did!—with the world.

Sometimes it takes years or even decades to find the courage to complete your book. Some of our authors have spent twenty years composing their memoirs, until something—including a terminal illness—prompts them to contact us and finally publish. This happened with one of our authors, who was able to give his beautifully designed hardcover memoir to family members at a gathering just months before he passed.

And sometimes we're just not ready to write the book because we're still learning, growing, and evolving. That was the case for Elizabeth with her Goddess Power book series, which took more than a decade to complete. During that time, she was using the tools that she teaches to do her own inner work to transform into the authority and proof that her method really works. That prepared her to publish her book series that guides women—as her motto promises—to "live bigger, better, and bolder, creating a personal and professional empire that you rule from a throne of power wearing a crown of confidence."

Consider time and timing. If you're consumed by something that profoundly occupies your time and energy, such as caring for an aging or ill parent, balancing a robust career with a busy family, facing a difficult obstacle such as divorce or grueling medical treatments, or celebrating an achievement such as opening a new business or earning a PhD, then you may not have the capacity to write a book right now. However, if you don't have extenuating circumstances, don't let "I don't have time" or "I'm too busy" stop you.

We all have twenty-four hours in a day. Many of our authors have written books despite busy travel and speaking schedules. When Elizabeth wrote her first bestselling novel, she was working full-time as a big-city newspaper reporter and planning her wedding. But she was *obsessed* with becoming a published author. So, she rose at 5 a.m. to write for a few hours before her demanding workday. On the weekends, she chose to write instead of going to the movies or parties. Years later, when she worked in an office, that dedication enabled her to complete her first screenplay.

You have to become **obsessed** with writing, publishing, and promoting your book. That's what it takes to summon the discipline and sacrifice—which is actually *investment* into your future—to make your book mission a success. Writing a book also requires courage and confidence.

Contemplate this as motivation: Your soul-deep calling to write a book is bigger than you. It's a life mission. It's a life assignment that you're supposed to complete.

We believe it's **a moral obligation** to fulfill this calling, because the book isn't just about you. It's about all the people in the world whose lives you can change—or even *save*—by sharing your story, experiences, and wisdom.

Analytics show that our books and our authors' books have readers on every continent and in places such as Madagascar and Morocco. While we and our authors may never go there, our books *are* there, touching lives and hearts, inspiring minds, and possibly changing and saving lives. That is power! But it won't happen if you don't finish your book.

The icing on the cake is that when you finish writing your book and actually get it published, you will feel an indescribable sense of accomplishment and joy. You can't put a dollar amount on the thrill of achieving something that most people dream about but never actually do. Sadly, we know many people who had fascinating stories and legacies, but took their books to the grave because they never committed to making it happen. Some were sidelined by illness, scandals, or circumstances that drained their time and energy until it was too late.

Don't let that be you. It's time to get obsessed!

This starts with a mindset shift.

So let's figure out what's been stopping you from writing your book. Exploring the 5 W's and H—Who, What, When, Where, How, and Why—will help you find the confidence and courage to write your book.

Write your answers and allow the questions to continue to percolate in your mind.

Who am I afraid will read my book and be critical and/or disapproving?

_____

_____

_____

_____

_____

When you reach the tipping point where your desire to write your book overpowers your concern about other people's opinions and potential criticism, your writing will flow like a river. How can you face the fear and release it, then psych yourself up to that tipping point and finally take action?

What consequences do I fear could occur from writing my book?

_____

_____

_____

_____

_____

It's legitimate to consider the consequences of publishing, say, an erotic novel under your name when you work in a reputation-sensitive field where that might tarnish your image. If that's your situation, then consider publishing the book with a pen name.

Likewise, many people fear exposing family secrets in a memoir, even when those secrets helped shape who they are. How can you tell your truth without incriminating people (unless that's your intent)? It's always best to consult with a lawyer so you understand the potential legal ramifications, if any, of what you write about other people.

When did I give up or convince myself my book will never happen?

_____

_____

_____

_____

_____

Did someone tell you that your book is an impossible dream? How many books have *they* written!? You can glean confidence from first-time authors who never thought they'd write a book, and they did!

Where are my anxiety, fear, and/or insecurity coming from?

_____

_____

_____

_____

_____

Get still and silent with yourself and meditate, pray, journal—whatever works for you—and really excavate the root cause of these feelings. You can even talk about it with a therapist. Until this is resolved, self-sabotage could very well be lurking and looking for a chance to pounce in the form of procrastination, leaving your book unwritten.

How can I convince myself that I'm safe to express myself and be vulnerable when writing my book?

_____

_____

_____

_____

_____

Talk with other authors about how they handled this. Besides exploring the question here, you can also journal with raw honesty and craft a strategy to psych yourself up to feel the fear and write your book regardless.

If **time** is my major obstacle, how can I carve out time and commit to a writing, publishing, and promotions schedule to maximize my book's success?

_____

_____

_____

_____

_____

Every day, we have the privilege of investing our minutes and hours—outside of time for work, family, fitness, and faith commitments—however we desire. So assess where and how you spend your time. Then shift your thinking to view your writing time as "investing" in your book project that will pay immeasurable dividends of personal satisfaction, professional elevation, global influence, financial abundance, and so much more.

Sometimes it's best *not* to publish a book at a particular time. For example, our mother chose to wait until her mother had passed before she published her 2017 book, *The Triumph of Rosemary: a Memoir* by Judge Marylin E. Atkins. Why? Because the book—which is now a screenplay intended for a Hollywood feature film—chronicles her mother's physical and psychological abuse. And our mother did not want to shame our grandmother in her golden years. Our mother had left the pain in the past. So she waited.

If you're going through extenuating circumstances such as medical treatments that leave you foggy and exhausted, or writing your dissertation, or taking care of a newborn, or moving to a new city to start a demanding job, then perhaps now is *not* the time to write your book. Give yourself grace. On the flip side, writing—even in short spurts—may provide a reprieve amidst chaotic or disorienting situations.

If you push pause for now, don't abandon your book forever. Commit to a date when you will start writing. Know, however, that life will always be presenting circumstances that provide easy and legitimate excuses to *not* write. That's why so many books are taken to the grave. Don't let that be you.

Why am I still thinking about and dreaming about my book, but not writing it?

_____

_____

_____

_____

_____

Writing is a Supernatural Superpower

Elizabeth describes her creative flow state as an out-of-body experience. It's as if a satellite dish is attached to her head, transmitting ideas into her brain, which makes her fingertips dance over the keyboard at lightning speed, while words stream across the screen. She becomes so entranced by this experience that she loses track of time and realizes the sun has set. Sometimes she jolts back into physical reality and realizes, *Oh wow, I'm sitting at my desk typing, and all these words are showing up in my book.*

Where are the words and ideas coming from?

Elizabeth believes that ideas and the specific way of expressing them all flow from supernatural sources. Call these sources God, the Universe, the cosmos, your Higher Self, or whatever aligns with your beliefs. Writers are artists, and while many are inspired by life experiences to write songs, paint, and create, a good portion of artists will credit a source greater than themselves, such as the ethers, Spirit, ancestors, angels, a divine muse, etcetera. These artists, including writers, feel like a vessel who receives messages that flow through them and they in turn become the messenger who shares this visionary information with people everywhere.

Some writers actually channel entire books that they receive in a "download" during meditation or while writing in their flow state. If you're not familiar, your **flow state** is that magical mental space where you're so immersed in your creativity that your inner critic goes silent, your mind is wonderfully focused, your ideas are connecting brilliantly, and you actually feel euphoric. You are in your genius zone. And you are finally *doing it!* Athletes also get into this zone of total concentration that engages their minds, bodies, and even superhuman energy.

Believe what you'd like, but we believe that writing is a supernatural act. It allows Spirit to channel messages through your intuition, which speaks through your inner voice. Then it's your job to bring those ideas into physical reality by writing them. The more you attune to this practice, the stronger your connection to this infinite source of ideas will become.

When you tap into this limitless creativity, you silence the noise of your thinking mind, along with your inner critic that may try to tell you that you're not smart enough to write a book, that it will fail, and that nobody will read it. This inner critic is a villain that has crushed many an author's dream and left their book unwritten. Likewise, when you dial into the frequency of a higher power, you'll muzzle the chorus of naysayers whose criticism and cynicism may be echoing in your thoughts when you sit down to write.

One way to strengthen your connection to this divine guidance and amplify its communications is to clear your energy and meditate each day, or as frequently as possible. This really works! Elizabeth does this and it makes magic happen for her writing. As a certified meditation teacher, she guides writers through this practice to help unleash their creative power.

If you want to tap into your most genius creativity and ascend into a flow state where time and space dissolve, consider the power of meditation to help get you there.

Please use this QR code to access Elizabeth's Guided Energy Clearing and Meditation for Writers. It will relax you, clear your mind, and help you write the best book possible.

Meditation for Writers

GET CLARITY

Write Your Summary Sentence

Know Your Intention, Your Why, and Your Target Audience

"Begin with the end in mind."
— Stephen Covey, *7 Habits of Highly Effective People*

Elizabeth conceived the "Summary Sentence" concept for her "Six Months to Bestselling Book Success" program when she began coaching people across America to write their memoirs, business books, and novels. This three-part sentence becomes the North Star that guides your book-writing journey.

It contains the guiding principles that motivate your mission. You wouldn't leave your home to visit a new destination without clear directions, so think of your Summary Sentence as your literary GPS. Without it, you may you risk getting lost, wasting time, meandering through frustrating detours, and even getting angry because your book is still not written.

Your Summary Sentence ensures that you follow the most direct, efficient, time-saving route to finish your book. Investing your brain energy into this exercise now enables you to compose your book in a way that speaks directly to your target reader with the most concise and impactful messaging that optimizes the long-term success of your publishing experience.

The following exercise often sparks a magical moment when an aspiring author suddenly shifts from overwhelm and confusion into clarity, confidence, and motivation to write.

Let's start by exploring how your Summary Sentence contains three parts: your Intention, your Why, and your Target Audience.

Set Your Intention

Your Intention is the big-picture goal for your book. It's the "wildest dream" version of what you envision as a published author. This is different for every writer. And *you* get to decide what it is, based on your individual values and goals.

So, when you think of your future self as a published author, what do you imagine as the biggest, best possible outcome? What do you want? Bestseller status? Millions of dollars from book sales and movie deals? Elevation as a thought leader? Awards and accolades? A Nobel Prize in Literature? A business book that boosts branding and attracts new customers? An interview with Oprah? Global travel as a high-paid speaker? Or simply touching one life at a time?

Write your Intention. Describe the greatest possible outcome and influence for your book.

_____

_____

_____

_____

_____

Recite this and rehearse it in your mind every day. Feel gratitude as if it's already your reality.

Know Your Why

Why do you want to write a book? For many authors, people have told them, "Your story is amazing! You should write a book!" so many times, that they finally take action and do it.

That was the case for Joanie Lindenmeyer, author of the 2023 bestseller, *Nun Better: An Amazing Love Story*, about how she was a Roman Catholic nun who fell in love with another nun, Carol Tierheimer, and they ultimately spent forty wonderful years together. Similarly, Dr. Robert Treuherz heard the same encouragement after his first of ten near-death experiences that he describes in his 2025 memoir, *Ten 2ⁿᵈ Chances: This Doctor Died and Went to Hell. Why?*

Our mother also heard the urgings so frequently that she finally sat down on her wedding anniversary in December of 2016 and by May of 2017, had completed *The Triumph of Rosemary: A Memoir* by Judge Marylin E. Atkins. Then readers said, "Your story should be a movie!" Hence, the screenplay.

Likewise, our author Judy Bohning, who survived multiple catastrophic experiences that include the MGM fire in Las Vegas, compiled them in *Memoirs of an Eccentric* in 2023, after many people encouraged her to write a book.

Your Why is a driving force for your book, and it will motivate you, especially if the writing gets tough or you question whether it's worth your time and effort. Yes, it is! Elizabeth wrote and published her 2018 memoir, *God's Answer Is Know: Lessons From a Spiritual Life*, because it was a spiritual calling to teach others how to meditate. Catherine composed The Veronica Series of novels that begin with *Hey Veronica, I Heard Your Mom's Black* to fill a void in the Young Adult market by showcasing a mixed-race girl navigating a world obsessed with race.

For several of our authors, their Why is to privately publish their life story to share only with family, friends, and close colleagues.

Your Why is deeply personal, so write it here:

_____

_____

_____

_____

_____

Define Your Target Audience

This is *everything.* You need to write your book as if you're talking directly to your ideal readers, because you *are.*

You want them to say, "I loved your book because it felt like you were having a conversation with me." That's what people often say about our mother's book.

To get there, start by thinking about how you naturally talk to the people in your life. At work, especially when speaking with executives or clients, you may keep your tone more formal. With lovers, best friends, and family members, you probably speak more freely and personally. And you probably express yourself differently with your grandparents than you do with children.

The key when writing a book is to know who you're "talking to." When you confuse, you lose, so your words must resonate with the reader.

For example, if you're a doctor writing a book for other physicians, you can use medical terms and lingo that they will understand. However, if you're a doctor writing a book for the general public, it's imperative that you write it in a way that we will understand. That means using everyday language and simple explanations for complex medical terms and concepts.

Likewise, if you're writing a romance novel, you need to understand what romance novel readers love in terms of characters, plot, setting, pacing, historical eras, and series. And if your romance novel is for a particular imprint at a big publishing house, you must understand their guidelines and follow them to a tee, because your audience in this context includes your literary agent and acquisitions editors who have the power to purchase your manuscript.

Two of our authors who are lifelong Detroit Lions fans became so exasperated with our losing team that they wrote books about it! Their Why was to express their anger and frustration after watching our home team fumble for decades despite the die-hard hope that they shared with millions of fans. And their Target Audience is comprised of people like themselves—people who can't escape their love-hate relationship with the Detroit Lions, and who can't shake the hope that *someday* our team can win a Super Bowl championship.

We are so proud of Barry Schumer's 2023 book, *I Don't Believe It! We're Good? The New Detroit Lions* and Mark McCarthy's 2025 book, *Armchair Assessments: Existing as a Lions Fan.* While writing, they "spoke" directly to their target audience, because they were living the experience along with them.

While many people love books about sports, a football book is not for everyone. This is an important message if you're like many authors who say, "I want *everyone* to read my book." Well, they won't. And sometimes an author actually tells readers that this book is *not* for you if you don't share certain beliefs.

U.S. Army Master Sergeant Cedric King, author of *The Making Point: How to succeed when you're at your breaking point*, tells readers in his best-selling 2019 memoir that it's not a book for them if they don't believe in God. Cedric credits God for his miraculous survival story: He stepped on a bomb in Afghanistan while leading troops, lost his legs, and now competes as a triathlete and inspires audiences across America as a motivational speaker.

Cedric turned his pain into a powerful platform to help others. And his grueling recovery blessed him with insights that form the foundation of lessons in his book and speeches. As a result, he references the power of God throughout his book.

Knowing your reader's "**pain points**" enables you to capture and keep their attention. To understand this concept, we highly recommend that you read *Building a StoryBrand: Clarify Your Message So Customers Will Listen* by Donald Miller and complete his exercises on how to craft messaging for your audience.

Your book solves a problem by addressing the reader's pain points. This can be as simple as providing a fantasy that helps readers escape from everyday reality. Or your book about how you survived a terminal illness may give hope to someone who receives a similar diagnosis. Likewise, your business book can share your lessons that help someone ascend from an entry-level position to the CEO chair.

Write a detailed description of your ideal reader, including: age range, gender, geographic location, socioeconomic status, health, education, interests, cares/concerns, passions, struggles, values, and pain points. You may even have a specific person in mind as you write, because they embody the "avatar" who is struggling with the challenges that your book can help them resolve.

_____

_____

_____

_____

_____

What problems will you help them solve with your book? List them below. Are you sharing your own story as a testimonial to inspire others that they can overcome a particular challenge? Are you offering "how to" guidance to achieve that?

_____

_____

_____

_____

What tone and writing style will best appeal to them? Describe them here. When you have a good understanding of who you're writing for, you'll know how to speak to them on the pages of your book.

_____

_____

_____

_____

What action steps do you want your readers to take? List them below. Do you want them to follow your guidance? Immerse in the story to relax and forget their worries? Feel inspired to sign up for your on-line coaching program that takes your book's instruction to the next level? Write an online review of your book? Use a coupon at the back of your book to visit your business?

_____

_____

_____

_____

Where can you find these readers in person and online?

Are they in groups on LinkedIn or FB? What hashtags can help you find them on social media?

Where do they congregate in person? A place of worship, the annual conferences for your profession or industry, conventions, networking groups, the country club/golf course, certain restaurants, the gym, yoga classes, cooking classes?

If your target audience is "divorcing/divorced people," as the upcoming example demonstrates, you could find them through divorce lawyers, support groups, hashtags pertaining to divorce, people in the comments of social media accounts that focus on divorce, conferences and events, etcetera.

_____

_____

_____

_____

What types of promotions will appeal to your readers?

_____

_____

_____

_____

Know the value of word-of-mouth! Ask trusted friends and colleagues how to connect to these people, and ask for referrals that provide entrée into their realms.

If your book is about personal financial empowerment, for example, you could team up with people in the banking/mortgage/credit business who may allow you to do a presentation for their customers or you could ask them to recommend your book to their customers (if allowed).

Write Your Summary Sentence

It's time to combine the above information into your Summary Sentence. As the guiding light on your book-writing adventure, it encapsulates the mission that's driving your story. It keeps you focused by:

1) Summarizing your **Why**;
2) Stating your **Intention**; and
3) Describing your **Target Audience**.

Here's an example of a Summary Sentence:

"This book enables me to *share my knowledge* after overcoming a painful divorce by writing my formula for healing and reinventing myself *to teach* other *divorcing/divorced people* how to do the same, and I want to *use the book as the curriculum for my online seminars and retreats*."

In this example, here are the three parts:

Why: share my knowledge and teach

Intention: use the book as the curriculum for my online seminars and retreats.

Target Audience: divorcing/divorced people

Let's Write Your Summary Sentence

Why I'm writing this book:

_____

_____

_____

My **Intention** is:

_____

_____

_____

My **Target Audience** is:

_____

_____

_____

Combine all of the above to write your **Summary Sentence** here:

_____

_____

_____

_____

_____

Post your Summary Sentence at the top of your manuscript. Print it and display it where you'll see it while composing your book. It will keep you focused to write the most concise, impactful book.

Use Creative Visualization to Achieve Your Success

You can use your imagination and your writing skills to manifest the best possible outcome for your book. This really works. Here's how.

When Elizabeth was writing her first novel, a romantic thriller, she envisioned herself sitting at a table in Borders bookstore, autographing her bestselling book while a long line of excited people waited to meet her and get a personal inscription in their hardcover copy. Elizabeth wrote this scene in great detail as if she were scripting it. She included dialogue from readers telling her why they loved the book, that it was a page-turner, that they had seen her on a TV interview, and that they had never read anything like her novel. Then she read the script aloud and recorded it into a microcassette recorder, and listened to it, over and over, while visualizing the scene and feeling the excitement, gratitude, and fulfillment of the experience.

And guess what? It happened!

Elizabeth did TV interviews and had many book signings in Borders, Barnes & Noble, Waldenbooks, and independent bookstores where people lined up to purchase autographed copies of her first, best-selling novel, then her second, and her third. This method combines creative visualization, scripting, and autosuggestion.

Elizabeth created this technique by combining what she learned from the book, *Creative Visualization: Use the Power of Your Imagination to Create What You Want in Your Life* by Shakti Gawain, along with the success book, *Think and Grow Rich* by Napoleon Hill. Then she combined the techniques into a method that has helped her write dozens of books, lose 100 pounds and get super fit, manifest vacations and material blessings, activate her Goddess Power, and experience miraculous healings in relationships.

How can you use this technique to manifest the greatest success for your book? Start with your Summary Sentence as the foundation. Then write your vision for you, your book, and its influence on the world. Compose a scene that exemplifies the excitement, prosperity, and accolades. Then read it aloud into the audio recording app on your phone. Listen to it, visualize the outcome, and feel the powerful emotions of this actually happening in 3D reality. Meanwhile, **do the work**, knowing that you *can* achieve anything that you conceive in your mind.

Carve Out Time & Space for Writing

It's best to prepare for your writing experience by designating time and space where your writing will happen.

Time: Look at your calendar and determine where and when you can carve out time for your writing. If your calendar is already jam-packed, can you delegate some responsibilities to others? What can you temporarily pause until your book is complete?

If it feels like sacrifice, think of it as an investment. And use our mantra: **"Fleeting pleasure, books forever."** This means you can spend a few hours or even a weekend having fun, but have nothing to show for it. Or you can invest the time into writing, and you'll have pages and chapters for your book, which lasts forever and benefits you in countless ways. It's your choice!

Find your writing rhythm: When do you have the highest energy and the best mental clarity for writing? Morning, afternoon, evening, the middle of the night? Before or after eating, exercising, sleeping, meditating, drinking coffee?

If you don't know, experiment. Then fiercely guard that time to invest in your writing. Don't schedule anything during those hours, turn off your devices, and find the discipline to use every ounce of energy to compose your book.

Space: Designate a private area where you can best focus and work without interruption. Make it clean and inviting with motivational notes, good music, supplies, technology, and comfort. De-clutter. Experiment with elements such as room temperature, lighting, aromatherapy, air flow, the ergonomics of your chair and desk, etcetera, to find your sweet spot. A cooler room with a ceiling fan circulating the air, or an open window with a fresh breeze blowing in, may enhance your mental energy and focus.

Stillness and silence: You can hear your all-knowing inner voice speak most clearly to express your ideas when you make a practice of getting still and silent, uninterrupted by people and devices. Create a pre-writing ritual that enables you to mentally unplug and mute the noisy world through meditation, journaling, a nature walk, or another mind-clearing activity. Some writers, however, love the noisy bustle of a coffee shop, or the blare of music while they're writing. Figure out what works best for you.

Lifestyle: Lifestyle is everything. You need sleep, water, high-vibe foods, exercise, and comfortable clothing. Experiment with each to determine your best formula for writing. The more you practice wellness for your body, the easier it will be for your mind and spirit to enter your genius zone.

Prepare to Write & Publish

Getting organized now will save you time and money, and spare you from misery. You won't waste time searching your computer for the latest version of your manuscript, because you'll easily access it in a folder with other materials. And you won't have to shuffle through stacks of papers on your desk searching for the notes you jotted down about the literary agent you heard about, because the notes will be in a labeled file folder.

Failing to get organized now could derail your writing by costing time and energy if you have to search for your work every time you sit down to write.

So please invest the time and effort right now to customize a system for your writing. If you prefer a paperless plan, then create folders on your computer and save them on your favorite **cloud-based online storage system** such as Google Drive, Microsoft OneDrive, and Dropbox. These systems allow you to store files—such as documents, photos, videos, spreadsheets, and PDFs—on the Internet instead of only on your computer. These platforms also let you share files with your editor, graphic designers, and other people on your book team. And you'll have peace of mind knowing that your materials are protected if your computer crashes or you accidentally delete your book files.

You can start by creating one main folder called, "My Book." Then inside, create three folders: Writing, Publishing, and Promoting. Keep every draft of your manuscript in the Writing folder. Any information you learn and need for publishing goes in the Publishing folder. Likewise, your Promoting folder contains information about your launch, including venues, publicists, podcasts that you want to be a guest on, etcetera. Then be diligent about transferring materials and information into each file, rather than letting them get lost on your desktop or in other folders.

If you prefer to use a pen to compose your book on paper, then keep your workspace stocked with pens and note pads. Use file folders labeled Writing, Publishing, and Promoting to store notes and research materials, and keep them in a neat container.

Select a Publication Date and Reverse Engineer Your Writing Time

If you're self-publishing or working with a hybrid publisher, you can select your publication date. However, if you're seeking representation by a literary agent with the hopes of landing a book deal with a traditional publishing company (we'll explain this later in detail), then your publication date could be years away, and your publisher will determine it.

So, if you have control over your publication date, now's the time to determine a meaningful day. It could be your birthday for a memoir, an anniversary for your business—like this book celebrates Two Sisters' ten-year anniversary—or a time when people focus on certain topics that are relevant to the content of your book.

This is a smart strategy because the media will be searching for story ideas on that topic and will be more likely to shine their spotlight on you for interviews, which help promote your book and boost sales. For example, if your book is about motherhood, then release it in time for Mother's Day and plan events around it, such as a brunch where each ticket includes an autographed book. Likewise, if you have a political book, you could time its release with an election cycle. If you're writing a love story, aim for Valentine's Day or the June wedding season, but find a unique angle so your book stands out during these competitive times.

Exactly how long will it take you to prepare for your publication date? Let's reverse engineer the process to strategize everything you need to do to reach that target publication date. It's time to do some math to calculate the time to research, write, publish, and promote at least four to six months prior to your book's release date.

Calculate Your Writing Time

Let's calculate how much time you'll need to compose and publish your book. Write:

1. The word count in your book: _____.

2. Your publication date:_____.

3. The amount of time you've allotted for writing (for example, six hours per week):_____.

If you have not allotted time, then these calculations will help you determine how much time to commit.

Next, time yourself while writing to calculate how long it takes you to complete two types of writing:

A) continuous writing from memory and/or imagination; and

B) research writing that requires consulting articles, journals, interviews, statistics, etc., that you must process and put into words to compose.

To do this, time yourself for five minutes doing each, and determine how many words you've composed. Your computer will provide a "word count." Simply highlight the passage, place your cursor on the tool bar at the top of your screen, scroll down to "word count," and click.

After continuous writing for five minutes, I wrote _____ words and _____pages.

After research writing for five minutes, I wrote _____ words and _____pages.

Note: a 200-page, 6x9" printed book is typically about 50,000 to 60,000 words, depending on font, spacing, and layout.

In the publishing industry, a standard manuscript page is formatted double-spaced in 12-point Times New Roman with one-inch margins and contains approximately **250 words per page.**

Now do some math.

If it takes you ____ minutes to continuously write one page, and ____ minutes to research-write one page, and your book is about half and half of each, then use those figures to calculate how many **hours** it will take you to actually write the book.

Then look at your publishing method and your publication date.

(Even if you don't know your publication date, you can still use this method to determine how long it will take to write your book. If you intend to work with a literary agent, for example, you can still set a deadline for yourself to finish your manuscript within, say, eleven months.)

So, now's the time to ask: Are you allowing enough time to write the book, allot adequate time for editing, preparing for publishing, planning your launch, and promoting to build a buzz before its release?

Example: You want to publish your book one year from now. You can continuously write five pages in an hour and research-write two pages per hour. Your book is half and half. And you want it to total 200 pages (with no photos). Here's your calculation.

100 pages divided by 5 pages an hour = 20 hours

100 pages divided by 2 pages an hour = 50 hours

Total: 70 hours

If you've allotted seven hours every week for writing (one hour each day), then you'll need ten weeks to write your book. Please note, this is only for *writing* your book. You'll need to do similar calculations for assembling your team that may include an editor, an agent, a publisher, a graphic designer, and a publicist. You'll also need to designate time for communications with them, as well as the intense process of reviewing and approving pdf and physical proofs that are generated prior to publishing.

For your writing schedule, add at least one month to make space for things in the "life happens" category, such as illness, a power outage, a family member requiring your attention, an unexpected trip, or an all-consuming project/presentation at your job.

Next, compute how much interviewing and/or research might be required, along with time for gathering any photographs, articles, videos, journals, captions, graphics, and other content required for the book. Consider any special circumstances, such as having historic family photos scanned by a trusted photography service to create high-resolution digital images for your book.

You may also need time to obtain permissions to reprint copyrighted materials that include:

- Excerpts from books
- Song lyrics
- Movie lines
- Photographs and graphics
- Quotes from published articles, websites, magazines, newspapers, movies, etc.

You must obtain written permission from the owner of any intellectual property that you want to reprint in your book. That means finding the appropriate contact person, then calling or emailing them, to acquire written permission. Sadly, this can take a long time to get a response—if you receive any response at all.

For one of our books, we quoted our author speaking in a documentary created by a major production company that aired on television. After months of trying to contact someone at the network, we finally did, and their answer was: *No, you cannot quote our documentary in the book.* So, we had to rewrite that entire passage. Fortunately, some of our authors have had quick success when seeking permissions from book publishers to reprint an excerpt from another author's book.

Sometimes this requires paying a fee—often an expensive one! So, calculate the time you'll need to find contacts and send emails as well. Major national newspapers require written permission to reprint excerpts from articles, and their fees are very high.

Some authors don't understand this legal requirement. We never take a risk, and neither should you. Imagine how you would feel if another author published an excerpt from *your* book in their bestseller, without asking your permission. It's not fair and it's not legal.

If you have questions about this or other legalities regarding your book, ask a lawyer.

We're including this point in the section about how much time to commit to writing and publishing, because you'll need to designate time for seeking permissions if necessary.

How to Select a Title for Your Book

Sometimes you just *know*. Other times, it pops up in conversation. Or a single sentence in your book inspires the title. Each of our authors have a unique story behind their book titles, and we hope these examples can inspire you to find the best one for your book.

The title for Tara Heaton's award-winning 2025 memoir, *Life Minutes: Igniting Joy from the Fire of Heartache* was inspired by her thirteen-year-old daughter's declaration: "I don't want to waste my *life minutes!*" while the family coped with older daughter Caroline's devastating epileptic seizures.

Cedric King's title popped up while we were interviewing him during the ghostwriting process, and he said, "I want to show people how to use their *breaking* point as their *making* point." *Boom!* As soon as he said it, he knew that was his title: *The Making Point.* It was an exciting moment that proves the power of creative synergy, which is the creative energy that sparks when two or more people work together on a book.

Al Allen named his memoir *We're Standing By* because, as a longtime legendary Detroit TV news personality, he repeated that phrase multiple times every day for decades. Roger Sippl named his 2021 poetry collection *In the Extra Years* because he cherishes the "extra years" that he's been living after surviving a potentially fatal diagnosis many decades ago.

Bestselling author Bethany Boik titled her 2023 book, *Diary of a Schizophrenic*, because it reads like a diary and contains actual excerpts from her personal journals, as well as artwork that presents visual images of the mental anguish she has endured since her diagnosis at age thirteen.

Likewise, Vernon Devers wrote his 2023 book about his late father's life, titling it *98 years, 11 months, 19 days* to celebrate the exact number of days that his dad lived.

Some titles are very straightforward, such as *Memories of My Life: Reflections of a Former Nun Led by the Spirit* by Rosie Robles. She was inspired to compose her 2024 book based on transcripts from a series of radio interviews.

Steve Bullock—the first Black interim president of the American Red Cross—named his 2018 book *My Name is Steve Delano Bullock: How I Changed My World and The World Around Me Through Leadership, Caring, and Perseverance.* The title references a time when Steve was a teenager in the Jim Crow South working a summer job at a hotel where the white manager didn't value or respect him and his co-workers enough to learn their names. Instead, he wrote on envelopes containing their weekly pay: John #1, John #2, and John #3. Now Steve's book proudly proclaims his full name, including "Delano," which his parents selected to honor President

Franklin Delano Roosevelt.

Sadly, Steve passed away on September 10, 2025. Now his memoir remains to celebrate his remarkable story of being born a sharecropper's son in segregated North Carolina and rising to become a highly respected global humanitarian.

Should You Copyright or Trademark Your Book Title?

Copyright does *not* protect book titles. Under U.S. copyright law, short phrases—including book titles—are considered too brief to qualify for copyright protection, so any author can legally use the same or a similar title for a different book.

Trademark *can* protect a book title—but only in specific situations. A single, standalone book title usually **cannot** be trademarked. However, a title **can** be protected by trademark if it's used as part of an ongoing brand—such as a **series title**, a **program**, or a **business identity** (for example, a book series, course, podcast, or coaching brand with the same name). Remember this:

- **A single book title is** not copyrightable, and usually not trademarkable.
- **A series or brand name** is potentially trademarkable if it identifies a source of goods or services.

Here's an example:

- *The Healer Inside You*—as a single book, this title has no copyright or trademark protection.
- *The Healer Inside You*—as a book series, podcast, or coaching program, this title may qualify for trademark protection.

Remember:

- Copyright protects the *content* of your book.
- Trademark protects the *brand* built around it.

How can you learn more? When naming your book, you can do a free search on USPTO.gov, the website for the U.S. Patent and Trademark Office. You'll want to search to learn whether another person or company owns the trademark to your title idea, and whether their ownership is "active" or "dead." Even if it says "dead," you should also do an online search to ensure that nobody is using that title for commercial use, which could constitute common-law trademark.

We are not lawyers. And it's complicated. So please consult with a trademark lawyer. And if you conceive a unique term that you want to trademark, invest in an attorney to handle your trademark filing.

Years ago, we learned the hard way by doing it *wrong*. Someone at the trademark office called to inform us of our error, that our trademark application would not be approved— and that we would *not* be refunded our *hundreds* of dollars in fees that we had paid. Lesson learned: we entrust all copyright and trademark matters to our brilliant trademark attorney Leah Halpert. Thank you, Leah!

We have trademarked our company name along with Two Sisters in relation to those words used with anything relating to writing and publishing. Our trademarks enable us to use the ® symbol after Two Sisters Writing & Publishing® and Two Sisters®. It means we own the trademarks, and no other person or company can use them. Elizabeth also trademarked her podcast, The Goddess Power Show with Elizabeth Ann Atkins®, and we trademarked our PowerJournal® book series. Thank you again, Leah!

What happens if you infringe on someone else's trademark? You may receive a "cease and desist" letter from their lawyer telling you to unplug your entire platform: your book on retail sites, your website, your social media, and all branding materials such as stationery, posters, business cards, etcetera. It is not worth the risk!

We know an author who marketed a book for *years* to a global audience, building an online community, website, beautiful branding, and endless networking to promote a self-help guide. Sadly, after the book's release, the author received a "cease and desist" letter stating that their title was infringing on a trademarked concept that someone else was already using. The author had to unplug the book entirely: stop sales, shut down the website, and re-brand *everything*. This is a tremendously expensive and devastating experience that can be avoided with market research *before* you invest money, time, and dreams into your book and brand.

So do your homework *before* you select your book title.

It's Not Just a Book. It's a Mission!

Your book can start a movement, and even dramatically change the course of history.

That's what happened after the publication of Harriet Beecher Stowe's 1852 novel, *Uncle Tom's Cabin*. At the time, Northerners were apathetic to the Civil War and the plight of enslaved people. Then Stowe's novel presented deeply personal and heart-wrenching stories about the horrors of slavery, and this humanized the brutal reality of what was happening in the South. This triggered compassion and outrage among Northern readers, motivating them to join the Union's fight to defeat the Confederates and win the Civil War, thus ending slavery, forever changing the course of American history.

Consider that Harriet Beecher Stowe's book achieved this eons before anyone had thought about today's digital world that transmits news around the world at lightning speed— with the power to galvanize support for causes with graphic videos and images.

Instead, a simple book—with black words on white pages—had the power to help eradicate the brutal institution of slavery.

You also have the power to "write the change" you want to see in the world. We believe this so deeply that Elizabeth's book-coaching program was once called "Write the Change" and used the hashtag #writethechange. This is a play on the quote, "Be the change you wish to see in the world," by Mahatma Gandhi, who was nominated several times for the Nobel Peace Prize and is one of history's greatest leaders of nonviolent resistance. He published his philosophies in the 1929 book, *The Story of My Experiments with Truth.*

That said, please understand that you may be writing much more than a book. You may be like many authors who believe it's a mission.

That's true for five female powerhouses who reached executive status in the energy industry. Our authors Joyce Hayes Giles, Carolyn Green, Telisa Toliver, Rose McKinney-James, and Hilda Pinnix-Ragland teamed up to write the 2019 anthology, *The Energy Within Us: An Illuminating Perspective from Five Trailblazers.* Their mission is to share their success stories—how they defied the odds and rose through the ranks to shatter the glass and Black ceiling in corporate America.

And their mission extends far beyond that. They want to provide opportunities for Black women to pursue careers in STEM—Science, Technology, Engineering, and Mathematics. Therefore, all proceeds from their book are allocated to an American Association of Blacks in Energy college scholarship fund that enables Black female students to study STEM.

Raising money for a cause related to your book is a popular concept with our authors.

When Dr. Herman Williams and his wife Jeannie served as co-chairs of the 2019 Middle Tennessee Heart Gala in Nashville, hundreds of attendees received copies of his 2017 memoir, *Clear! Living the Life You Didn't Dream Of,* which chronicles his near-death experience after cardiac arrest. The event raised a record-breaking $1.3 million for the American

Heart Association.

In Texas, celebrity plastic surgeon Thomas J. Jeneby, MD, donates a portion of his book sale proceeds to **Family Violence Prevention Services, Inc.** in San Antonio. This is part of his philanthropic commitment to provide free reconstructive and cosmetic surgery for women who have been badly scarred by domestic violence. He writes about this mission in his bestselling 2019 book, *Confessions of a Plastic Surgeon: Shocking Stories About Enhancing Butts, Boobs, and Beauty.*

Education about history can be another mission that inspires your book. Elaine Makas, PhD, wants young people to learn about World War II, the horrors of Nazi Germany, and the brave efforts of soldiers who helped liberate Europe and defeat fascism. So, she penned the award-winning book, *A Young Man on the Front Line: Lessons of War*, which chronicles her father's true story as an eighteen-year-old soldier in the U.S. Army while liberating France and Germany from Nazi occupation during the 1940s. She wrote the book using her late father's actual wartime journals, and takes the reader through deadly battles, humorous moments, nightmarish scenes at Nazi death camps, and poignant moments between soldiers.

Dr. Makas markets the book to middle school and high school social studies teachers so that they can use her father's story to teach young people about this important part of American and world history through her father's voice and experience.

From First-Time Author to Radio Show Host!

Our bestselling author Joanie Lindenmeyer—a former Catholic nun and retired physical education teacher—wrote her 2023 memoir, *Nun Better: An Amazing Love Story*, about how she fell in love with another nun at the convent and ultimately enjoyed a forty-year romance and marriage with Carol Tierheimer after they both left the church.

At first, Joanie's mission was simply to share their unique and courageous story, which is very inspiring and entertaining. However, during her promotional events, many LGBTQ+ people shared deeply personal stories and questions with her. They especially wanted to know how to cultivate a spiritual life after the trauma of condemnation, shame, guilt, and rejection from traditional religion and their families.

These questions inspired Joanie to team up with Elizabeth to write two self-help books: *Joyously Free! Stories & Tips for LGBTQ+ People, Parents and Allies,* published in June of 2024 and launched at Motor City Pride in Detroit and at the Pride event in Brookings, Oregon, where Joanie lives. This book offers upbeat guidance on how to come out, live out and proud, support queer children at any age, and become an ally. *Joyously Free* also includes stories written by thirty-two contributors across America, who reveal their stories as queer individuals, as well as parents of and allies for LGBTQ+ people. This unique self-help book contains QR codes to Elizabeth's guided meditations, as well as writing exercises for self-exploration. Elizabeth and Joanie have used the book as a guide at many events that feature meditation, prayer, journaling, and conversations that help people heal and feel empowered.

They continued this mission in October of 2024, when we published *Healing Religious Hurts: Stories and Tips to Find Love and Peace* by Elizabeth Ann Atkins and Joanie Lindenmeyer, launched at Ashland Pride in Oregon and at a book party at the beautiful Paschal Winery & Vineyard in Southern Oregon wine country. This book has opened the doors for many speaking events at churches and other religious and spiritual groups.

When we say, "It's not just a book. It's a mission!"—that couldn't be more true for Joanie, whose outspoken visibility as a bestselling author landed her the amazing opportunity of hosting a weekly radio program called "Joyously Free with Author Joanie Lindenmeyer" on KCIW on the Curry Coast

Community Radio. The program explores topics relating to LGBTQ+ people, church, religion, and spirituality. When Joanie started writing her first book in Elizabeth's book coaching program, she had no idea that she would become a radio show host and popular speaker.

Likewise, Elizabeth's six-part Goddess Power book series forms the foundation for her life mission to empower women and people everywhere through mindset shifts, spiritual connection, self-discovery, and inner peace. She does that with *The Biss Tribe: Where You Activate Your Goddess Power,* *The Biss Tribe: Where You Activate Your Goddess Pleasure*—both published in 2024—and *The Biss Tribe: Where You Activate Your Goddess Prosperity*, coming in 2026. The next three books explore Protection, Peace, and GoddessLife. The books inspired her podcast, The Goddess Power Show with Elizabeth Ann Atkins®, her weekly Goddess Power Meditation for women across America and beyond, and her Goddess Power Retreats, most recently held for four days for nine women in the Dream House at Paschal Winery. The experience was magical—four rainbows appeared in a single day as we meditated, cleared our energy, and shared a soulful sisterhood.

Likewise, your book or books can amplify a life mission that already drives your work in the world. That's true for our author Jack Cooper, whose book, *Pain Before the Rainbow; a biomythographical anthology*, became a bestseller after its release for Pride in June of 2025. His mission as an award-winning author has been to use writing as a healing tool for himself, and reading as a healing tool for those who experience his poignant stories.

Writing About Mental Health as a Healing Mission

The Miser brothers are living proof that books can be so much more than ink on paper—they can be a ministry, a lifeline, and a living testimony. As such, their mission is to shine a compassionate light on mental illness by sharing Wendel Miser's remarkable triumph over a devastating schizophrenia diagnosis that once threatened to define his future.

In their first book, *A Valiant Battle: A Journey with Schizophrenia*, which we published in 2022, Wendel and his brother James opened their hearts to the world, chronicling a deeply personal journey that honors the power of family, faith, and love in the healing process. They continued this sacred work in 2023 with *Markers on the Way to God: God's Grace Transforming Mental Illness*, and in 2024 with *Meditations of a Healed Mind: Welcoming into God's Grace, Prayers and Invitations*. Each book features a prayerful, poetic voice that reveres Jesus and glorifies God's restoring presence.

Now, with their fourth book scheduled for release on Easter Sunday 2026, the Miser brothers continue to offer hope, healing, and holy encouragement to every reader who needs to know that restoration is possible—and that no one walks their journey alone. We are so proud to publish their four books, with possibly more on the horizon.

Similarly, our bestselling author Bethany Boik has been invited to speak about her decades-long struggle with schizoaffective disorder at Stanford University and for the Michigan chapter of the National Alliance on Mental Illness, the country's largest grassroots mental health organization. Elizabeth also interviewed Bethany on the Emmy-nominated TV show, *MI Healthy Mind*, which Elizabeth has been co-hosting with Michael Hunter since April of 2015, exploring mental health topics that aim to shatter the stigma and inspire people to get help. Bethany's interview has more than 209,000 views. And her 2023 book, *Diary of a Schizophrenic*, provides an important credential for Bethany's mission to educate people about mental illness and provide hope that healing and a productive life are possible.

Showcase Your Against-the-Odds Success

We have discovered something beautiful and consistent about the authors who find their way to us—they want to share what we lovingly call *Against-the-Odds Success Stories*. This is our specialty.

Again and again, we organically attract people whose lives are living proof that circumstances do not define destiny. One of the most inspiring examples is the remarkable story of Roy Roberts, who rose from poverty and racial oppression in the segregated South to become the highest-ranking Black executive in the global automotive industry. Elizabeth ghostwrote his memoir, *My American Success Story: Always the First, Never the Last*, which Roy published with journalist and author Anthony Neely in February of 2015. The book chronicles how Roy relied on education, perseverance, and faith to become a powerful vice president at General Motors. Roy's book continues to uplift, motivate, and remind readers everywhere that extraordinary success is possible, no matter where you begin.

It's Never Too Late to Write a Book

If you're worried that it's too late to write your book, it's not!

Our author Mary Jean Teachman proves that with her book, *There Is Gold in the Golden Years: A Memoir*, which we published in 2022.

"I'm writing this book through the eyes of a 90-year-old woman," she wrote in her Introduction.

This line made Elizabeth gasp and tear up when she first read the manuscript that recounts Mary Jean's amazing life that spans from the despair of domestic abuse and divorce, to the glamour of being a fashion model, to the devastation of losing two adult children, to the joy of finding lasting love with her second husband, Gerard Teachman. We published his memoir, *A Different Drummer: My Life as a Peacetime*

Soldier, alongside Mary Jean's as a beautiful companion piece, reminding us that your story matters at every age, and that you can share your legacy together.

We hope that this amazing couple inspires you to write your book now, because it's never too late—until it is. So please, start writing now!

SECTION 2

ORGANIZE & OUTLINE

You probably wouldn't drive cross-country without a roadmap or clear directions, so you shouldn't write a book without an outline. So now's the time to chart your course. This will help you avoid unnecessary pitstops and delays that waste time and energy, so you can stay focused on your topic and only include content that whisks your reader into their desired destination of reading a phenomenal book.

BOOK STRUCTURE

How to Organize the Content of Your Book

Memoir · Business Book · Novel

This is *your* book, and you have the creative power to organize and structure it however you desire. This is especially true if you're self-publishing or working with a hybrid publisher. However, if you're publishing with a traditional publisher, you may have to follow their guidelines for your genre. So, understand their requirements *before* you start writing.

If you plan to self-publish or work with a hybrid publisher or indie press, you still need to decide how to present your content before the writing begins. This includes writing an outline, which we'll explore shortly. Your outline is your literary navigation system that takes you on the most direct, fast, and efficient route from idea to published book.

That's why it's imperative that you select the structure of your book as the container that holds your story and/or information together so that readers can easily consume, digest, and retain it.

On a quick side note, we know many writers who are self-described **"pantsers."** That means they write "from the seat of their pants." In other words, they make it up as they compose their books. If that's your style, go for it. However, as college English majors who wrote countless papers with traditional outlines, we suggest that you use an outline to write your book.

So, let's explore the best ways to structure your memoir, business book, or novel.

Memoir: Organizing Your Life Story

We believe that everyone should write a memoir!

Composing your life story in your own words is a powerful celebration of all that you've survived and accomplished. It's a profound journey of self-exploration and empowerment. It is therapeutic and healing. It boosts your confidence and alters your perception of yourself and your life. Writing your memoir *will* change you—and forever preserve your legacy.

But what exactly is a memoir?

It comes from the French word, *mémoire,* which means memory or reminiscence, and it's a collection of stories from a person's life all woven around one or several themes.

You can write many memoirs, each exploring different themes. In fact, Maya Angelou wrote seven memoirs that comprise one of the most influential collections of a life story in American literature. When you carefully select your themes and relevant stories, this helps you decide *what belongs* and *what to save for another book.*

A memoir is not an autobiography, which is a linear chronicle of one's life from birth to present. While an autobiography is an entire life, a memoir is a slice of life. Its themes can expand across a lifetime or for a specific period. For example, one year in *Eat, Pray, Love* by Elizabeth Gilbert, or a solo journey in the wilderness in *Wild: From Lost to Found on the Pacific Crest Trail* by Cheryl Strayed.

Similarly, our author Gerard Teachman showcases a formative era of his life in his 2022 memoir, *A Different Drummer: My Life as a Peacetime Soldier,* by describing his years as a soldier, but not the following decades as a university professor.

And Carol Beth Nelson, MD, shares her riveting life story within the deeply personal context of a twenty-four-year marriage in *We Are Alike—A Memoir: How A Doctor Leveraged Her Neuroscience Expertise to Survive and Heal from Narcissistic Abuse.* Her bestselling 2025 book focuses on the marriage and her courageous healing journey, while only describing her medical career or professional achievements as they pertain to the marriage, divorce, and path to freedom, peace, and love.

When you write your memoir, you're following an ancient tradition. Memoirs date back to ancient times, including stories about war written by Julius Caesar (100-44 BC). The first memoir by a woman was *Revelations of Divine Love* by Julian of Norwich in the 1400s.

Here are examples of powerful and popular memoirs:

Walden: Life in the Woods by Henry David Thoreau

I Know Why the Caged Bird Sings by Maya Angelou

Eat, Pray, Love by Elizabeth Gilbert

Becoming by Michelle Obama

Angela's Ashes by Frank McCourt

Borderlands / La Frontera: The New Mestiza by Gloria Anzaldúa

The Blue Jay's Dance: A Memoir of Early Motherhood
   by Louise Erdrich

The Color of Water by James McBride

Dust Tracks on a Road by Zora Neale Hurston

How to Structure Your Memoir

How should you structure your memoir? Here are some ideas. Keep in mind that you want to demonstrate how you *changed* by resolving inner conflicts and/or overcoming major obstacles to achieve the peace/success/wisdom that you enjoy now. Everything is relative. Simply *surviving* a traumatic experience—such as domestic violence or a scandal leading to career loss—*is* the story. When you write about it, you'll see that you're a survivor and that you *are* enough. Sharing this story will affirm others with similar experiences and empower them to persevere as you did.

Here are some structures that you can use.

FAVORITE MEMOIR STRUCTURES

The Chronological Memoir. This is the most common.

- A chronology from birth to present-day life.
- Ideal for coming-of-age stories, healing journeys, and long transformations.
- Easiest to compose.

Example structure:

- Part I: Before
- Part II: The Major Life Turning Point
- Part III: After

Here's an example:

- Part I: Feeling "different" and ostracized as a child
- Part II: Coming out as gay in college
- Part III: Becoming an international activist for LGBTQ+ freedoms

Our extraordinary author Elmer Dixon organized his bestselling 2023 memoir, *Die Standing: from Black Panther Revolutionary to Global Diversity Consultant*, in three parts: Childhood & Family, The Black Panther Party, and Life After The Party. Three photo galleries separate each section. Elmer is a popular speaker around the world and his TEDx Talk on YouTube is titled, "Stories from the revolution's front lines." Readers rave about being inspired and enthralled by his powerful life story.

Here's another structure example:

- Part I: The Struggles
- Part II: The Healing & Awakening
- Part III: The New Era of Empowerment

This might look like:

- Part I: Raised in an impoverished and abusive family of drug addicts.
- Part II: You escape and cut ties with hurtful people who won't change.
- Part III: You create a stable, prosperous life, career, marriage, and family.

Our author Sylvia Mustonen, DO, follows this format in her robust 2023 memoir: *New Medicine for a New Millennium: A Memoir Looking Front to Back in Time at a Black Woman's Life in Medicine.* She weaves her deeply personal story through her ascent in the medical profession, demonstrating her resilience and resourcefulness while facing racism, sexism, divorce, and other challenges, and how she ultimately found peace and joy.

Similarly, Alma G. Stallworth, PhD, a longtime member of the Michigan of House Representatives, shared her life story in her 2018 memoir, *Legacy of a Lawmaker: Inspired by Faith & Family.* Her legacy included founding the Michigan Legislative Black Caucus Foundation. She passed away in 2020 at age eighty-seven.

The Thematic Memoir. This is ideal if you want to explore a specific angle of your life.

- Structured around themes rather than time.
- Each chapter explores a different aspect of your experience.
- Time may hopscotch around your lifetime.
- Provides the ability to dive deep into important topics

Example themes:

- Identity
- Love
- Loss
- Power
- Healing

For instance, Elizabeth structured her memoir around four formative themes: food and fat, divorce, fear, and racial identity/religion. She actually combined many of the structural elements presented here, and organized the material in three sections comprised by vignettes. The story arc began with struggles that led to a scary turning point/awakening, and opened the door for the peace and success that she enjoys today.

If this appeals to you, then list the major themes that you'd like to use as the foundation of your memoir.

Theme #1_____.

Theme #2_____.

Theme #3_____.

Theme #4_____.

You can also list all the stories that support each theme. Do this on paper or on a computer, and refer to them when you create your outline.

The Vignettes Memoir is perfect if you think in snapshots, bullet points, or a series of social media posts that tell a story over time.

- Short, self-contained scenes or snapshots.
- Each piece stands on its own but contributes to a larger story.

- Perfect for reflective or poetic memoirs.
- Fun and simpler to write.
- Today's readers love a quick story.

Our author Al Allen wrote his unique 2018 memoir, *We're Standing By*, as a collection of vignettes that read like broadcast news stories, each celebrating his pioneering life and legendary career as a TV news personality in Detroit, Michigan.

Al's book emphasizes an important point: you are free to write as much or as little as you desire. While Elmer's book exceeds 400 pages, Al capped his memoir at seventy-six-pages! Many people asked him to expand it, but he was resolute in saying:

"No, this is my story and this is how I want to tell it!"

Sadly, Al (whose official name was Andrew Tyrie Long) passed on February 4, 2025, at age seventy-nine. It was so beautiful at his funeral when former Fox 2 News anchor Sherry Margolis held up his book and celebrated the fact that Al's memoir will continue to celebrate his legacy.

Your Business Book: Organizing Ideas for Influence

Your business book can elevate you as a leader in your field, boost your branding, and establish you as the "go to" expert because you literally "wrote the book" on what you do. Very importantly, your business book can share your expertise and help people who need it most.

This was the motivation for our author, Francisco Arredondo, MD. He is a very successful entrepreneur who founded fertility clinics and other businesses based in Texas. He wanted to solve the problem for physicians who believe they are not good businesspeople, even though running a medical practice *is* a business. He also recognized that medical schools were not teaching business basics, and he wanted to help physicians and medical workers master entrepreneurial skills. So, Elizabeth ghostwrote and we published his book, *MedikalPreneur: The Official Guidebook for Physicians' Success in Business.* This 2022 release shares his life story that inspired his mission, along with his solid business lessons that specifically address medical professionals.

Similarly, Elizabeth is ghostwriting a book for an extremely successful entrepreneur who is sharing his success secrets that he learned from his parents and grandparents; now those philosophies and practices form the foundation for his company's award-winning achievements and community enrichment.

In this type of business book, the best way to organize your content is to devote a chapter to each success secret, lesson, or challenge, then provide clear instructions for the reader to follow. Include anecdotes, statistics, and tips that help your readers understand and apply your teachings.

Before you get started, you may be asking, *what exactly is a "business book?"*

What Is a Business Book?

It's nonfiction that aims to **teach, guide, or inspire readers to upgrade their methods of working, leading, earning, or building something**—whether that's a company, a career, a brand, a lifestyle, or a professional life.

Our author Dr. Eduardo M. Sanchez teamed up with us to write and publish *Ask Dr. Ed, Baby's First Year: A Survival Guide for New & Experienced Parents*, an instructional book that helps parents nurture a baby from birth to age twelve months. Published in 2020, this book also showcases Dr. Sanchez's expertise and builds his brand as a beloved and trusted medical professional in San Antonio, Texas.

Unlike memoirs or novels, a business book focuses on the reader. It tells a story from a space of expertise and experience while providing **value** as strategy, framework, tools, rules, wisdom, or lessons the reader can apply in real life.

Popular Structures for Business Books

Which one is best for you? Get creative with how you structure your business book!

As the perfect example, please read the bestselling book, *Take the Helm: Navigating Your Way to Financial Freedom* by Roland Ghazal, a very accomplished financial professional and managing partner for a Fortune 100 company for several decades.

This 136-page book is entertaining to read while you learn exactly what he promises in the title. Roland brilliantly structured seven basic concepts about financial empowerment around the theme of "sailing the seven seas of life" with the goal of arriving at your own "paradise island." The metaphor puts an engaging spin on content that in too many financial books could come across as complicated or dull. Not this book! Roland masterfully balances humor, playfulness, and extremely solid financial guidance that really works. Each chapter explores a financial topic such as "Increase Your Work Value" and represents one of the seven seas of life. He also shares his personal story about how he became self-made through education, dedicated work, discipline, and integrity.

We are so proud to publish Roland's 2020 hardcover, paperback, eBook, and audiobook.

So, how will you structure your business book? Here are some ideas.

The Classic Business Book: the Problem → Solution → Result Structure

This works because it aligns with how readers face their challenges.

Start by identifying a problem that immediately resonates with your reader. Then explain why that problem exists and set the record straight on why past ideas and fractured systems are not effective. Lastly, present your solution and show what's possible when it's applied.

Examples of this structure include the runaway bestsellers: *Atomic Habits by James Clear, The 4-Hour Workweek by Timothy Ferriss, You Are a Badass by Jen Sincero,* and *Rich Dad Poor Dad by Robert T. Kiyosaki.*

This structure is ideal for your book if you're a coach, consultant, or expert who helps people solve a specific problem.

Share Your System: the Framework or Method-Based Structure

You built a business, reached the pinnacle of success, and now you want to share that with others who aspire to emulate your achievement. This concept is a very common and popular foundation for business books.

You do this by presenting your signature framework that distinguishes your brand and resulted in your wins. Your results-driven steps, pillars, principles, or an acronym usually form your framework. Then you showcase each concept in a chapter which builds on the previous one, leading the reader through a complete process.

This structure is clean, teachable, and highly scalable for courses, workshops, and coaching programs. Popular Detroit entrepreneur Regina DuBose celebrated thirty-five years in business by sharing her framework in *Perpetuating Wealth: Secrets to Longevity in Small Business.* Her 2021 book fortifies her mission to help small business owners succeed. In it, she courageously shares how she faced and resolved crises, and weaves solid advice around a smart framework that really works.

Similarly, after Elizabeth learned how to meditate and combined it with journaling for extremely powerful transformation, we created the first in a series of workbooks called *PowerJournal.* In 2018, we published *PowerJournal Workbook #1: A 28-Day Challenge,* and *PowerJournal Workbook #2: A 28-Day Challenge for Weight Loss* followed in 2019.

Similarly, our author and gym owner Anthony Moses created a workbook that helps people cultivate wellness called *A.M. Total Being Fitness: Creating Balance*, which we published in 2019.

Reveal Your Transformation Model: the Before → During → After Structure

Here's how you can escort your reader through your real-life journey, so they experience the change while learning your tools for their own transformation.

You start with a relatable failure, then transport them into the muck to explore where, how, what happened, and why. Then you describe the revelations and action steps that lead to a better place. This method fuses stories with strategy so your readers join your journey and see their own potential in your success.

Wealth coach Kathy Kali beautifully demonstrates this in her book, *Give, Save, Spend: How to Build Wealth and Change the World*, which is required reading in her coaching courses. She takes the reader through her own wealth journey—from the traumas to the hard lessons learned to the empowerment of teaching how she thrives. (We did not publish her book, but she wrote it during Elizabeth's "6 Months to Bestselling Book Success" coaching program.)

This format works well for your transformational story. A deeply inspiring example is *Lifted: A Journey from Trauma to Triumph* by Mike Ritter. His 2019 memoir shares how he evolved from a motorcycle gang member who'd suffered childhood traumas, into a very successful businessman who found solace in sailing and sailed around the world with his family. Mike invites the reader to experience the raw reality of his life before finding peace and purpose, all of which he eloquently weaves around the adventure and tranquility of sailing life.

A Two Sisters Favorite—The Hybrid: Life Story + Business Book

This is where memoir merges with strategy. We call this a "how-to memoir" and it's very popular. Our authors may not label it as such, but they organically conceive the concept and execute it beautifully. Such is the case with Dr. Arredondo's book, MedikalPreneur.

This structure weaves the author's personal stories with business lessons. Each chapter often starts with a relevant anecdote and ends with insight, reflection, or action steps.

For example, Herman Williams, MD, suffered cardiac arrest at age thirty-one while on the cusp of living his dream as an orthopedic surgeon for elite athletes. His near-death experience and the grueling, years-long recovery robbed him of that dream. As a result, he reinvented himself as a prominent hospital executive, all the while conceiving a framework to help people cope with catastrophic experiences. The Kindness Scale was born, and it's the final section of his 2017 book, *Clear!: Living the Life You Didn't Dream Of*. Now Dr. Williams uses the book as the foundation for his motivational speaking events and for his instruction as a consultant.

When you compose a "how-to memoir," your dramatic storytelling captures the reader's heart and inspires them to cheer you on through your recovery. That builds credibility for you as the author to teach your lessons learned amidst the trauma and grit of your experiences.

Kristy Sidlar does this beautifully in her bestselling book, *Change of Heart: My Journey of Transplantation, Revelation & Transformation*. With humor and heartfelt personal details, she takes the reader through her story of a happy life disrupted by a diagnosis that ultimately leads to a heart transplant. Her 2022 book concludes with a teaching section in which Kristy encourages readers to cultivate overall wellness, with a special focus on heart health. Kristy has shared this message through a TEDx Talk, in-person workshops, and speaking engagements.

After witnessing vast health care inequities in the insurance coverage and treatment she received as a prominent state lawmaker compared to her elderly mother, Alma G. Stallworth, PhD, published a second book with us in 2018: *Broken Hearts: Like Mother, Like Daughter: A Spiritual Call for Equality in Health Care.*

Your Hybrid: Life Story + Business Book or "how-to memoir" can explore any topic. Our author Regina DuBose wrote *Getting Started with Jesus: The Process for Spiritual Growth and Maturity* to share her personal story and steps for readers to follow to cultivate stronger faith.

This format fosters deep emotional connections between you and the reader, who becomes eager to learn how you persevered through a life-threatening experience and came out with joy and gratitude.

This is a great structure for you if you have a fascinating life story that inspired and/or directly relates to your business philosophy and what you teach.

Here are some of the most popular and successful business books.

Think and Grow Rich by Napoleon Hill
Lean In: Women, Work, and the Will to Lead by Sheryl Sandberg
The 7 Habits of Highly Effective People by Stephen R. Covey
Radical Candor: Be a Kick-Ass Boss Without Losing Your Humanity by Kim Scott
How to Win Friends & Influence People by Dale Carnegie
Dare to Lead: Brave Work. Tough Conversations. Whole Hearts. by Brené Brown
Start With Why by Simon Sinek
Rich Dad Poor Dad by Robert T. Kiyosaki
The 48 Laws of Power by Robert Greene
Winning by Jack Welch & Suzy Welch

Girl Code: Unlocking the Secrets to Success, Sanity, and Happiness for the Female Entrepreneur by Cara Alwill Leyba
Bossypants by Tina Fey
The Big Leap by Gay Hendricks

If you're writing a business book, study the examples on this list for how to effectively present business and teaching concepts. Pay attention to each book's content, structure, style, and tone.

Some of the most popular business books—including *Lean In*, *Dare to Lead*, and *Radical Candor*—become staple reads in corporate training, MBA programs, and leadership curriculums. That could be *your* book when you identify a void in the market and flex your expertise in a way that resonates with your target audience.

Novel: Organizing Your Story

Novels are built on events, scenes, and character change, all of which make your story feel *alive.* Structure keeps readers turning the pages as your story flows through a solid framework.

Common Novel Structures

The Three-Act Structure organizes your story in three parts:

- Act I: Setup
- Act II: Conflict and confrontation
- Act III: Climax and resolution

You can find the Three-Act Structure in plays, poetry, novels, comic books, short stories, video games, and movies. It was used in Shakespeare plays, Aesop's fables, Aristotle's poetry, and Hitchcock films. Hollywood and Broadway use it well. It's a solid structure because every act heightens the conflict and drama, which engages the reader's emotions, which keeps them reading until the end. This classic structure works for most genres.

The Hero's Journey is all about a life-changing challenge, transformation, and lessons that can be shared.

- The protagonist leaves their ordinary world.
- Experiences a call to adventure.
- Faces challenges that include "the dark night of the soul."
- Has a transformation.
- Returns empowered with lessons to teach.

The Hero's Journey is a gold-standard model for life showing your character's evolution. It comes from Joseph Campbell's 1949 book, *The Hero with a Thousand Faces*. He created this structure for storytelling; the story of Moses is an excellent example of The Hero's Journey.

Linda Lochard follows this format in her 2021 novel, *Life Along the Applegate Trail: A Tale of Grit and Determination*, which was inspired by her real-life re-enactment of a wagon-train journey on this rugged route into Oregon. The widowed heroine of her story experiences The Hero's Journey by embarking on the grueling and dangerous trip, then finding community and lifelong love.

Another historical novel based on real-life events is *Beyond That Room* by Susie Ruth Powell. Published in 2025, the fictional story takes place during the 1898 Wilmington Massacre in North Carolina. Susie's mission is to educate readers about this event through her dramatic, heart-wrenching story about a family facing frightening obstacles and tragedies with resilience and love.

The Hero's Journey follows a story arc, an important element for structuring your story.

Understanding Story Arc

You're taking your reader on a journey that includes the following:

- Starting Point: The story introduces the characters, plot, setting, themes, etc.
- Rising Action: The plot thickens. Think of climbing a mountain.
- Climax: The chase, the explosion, the battle. At the peak.
- Falling Action: Think of descending a mountain.
- Resolution: Resolving loose ends, concluding the story. Back on solid ground.

Create Character Profiles

When you're writing fiction, you need to create **a character profile** that includes personality traits, their appearance, and the formative moments that propelled them on their life trajectory. In this profile, include your character's favorite foods, biggest dreams, worst fears, pet peeves, quirky habits, personal style (clothing, hair, make-up, tattoos, piercings, etc.), favorite sayings, best childhood memories, most traumatic experiences, favorite season, preferred music, etc.

If you feel stuck on brainstorming these details, think about your sibling or best friend or lover/partner/spouse, and how you know every detail about them—including things that you love and others that may irritate you. Your characters should be imperfect, because that's how real people are.

You can write this profile as a list, a paragraph, a spreadsheet—whichever format works best for your creative flow. You'll want to reference it while writing, so make it legible, accessible, and easy to use. Here's where it gets really fun! You can use some of these traits as dramatic sparkplugs that ignite conflict in your story.

For example: You reveal that, since childhood, your character has been intolerant of people who chew with their mouths open and smack their food. This is an actual condition called Misophonia, a neurological and emotional response in which certain everyday sounds trigger intense irritation, anxiety, disgust, or even anger. Foreshadow this early in the story by showing, for example, your character storming out of the silent lunchroom at work because her supervisor is loudly crunching chips. This noise registers in your character's ears as if the supervisor is chewing into a microphone and the chomping sounds are amplified at maddening levels, triggering overwhelming agitation. However, your character wants to remain polite to her boss, despite the rage burning within. So, she makes an excuse about needing to return to her desk, gathers up her lunch, and hurries out of the lunchroom into the silent relief of her own cubicle.

Now that you've established your character's disdain for loud eaters, here's where the magic happens. This insight becomes inside information between you and your reader. So, plot that your character meets the person of her dreams, who invites her on a first date at her favorite romantic restaurant. Everything is blissful—until the food arrives. Because her date has the table manners of a farm animal: slurping their soup, smacking their food, chewing with their mouth open, and loudly licking their fingers.

The sight and sound make every cell inside your character's body prickle with agitation. Disappointment spirals through her; she wants to cover her ears and run away.

"Why aren't you eating?" the date asks. "Are you alright?"

No! She's not! And the reader knows, *this is a deal breaker*. It creates internal drama because your character really liked this person. It also triggers suspense that leaves the reader guessing how your character will react.

Remember to foreshadow your character's condition well before the dream date, and anticipate your reader's questions, such as, *why doesn't she just tell the person that she has this* condition, and if they want to be with her, they need to improve their table manners.

Then you can provide deeper insight into your character. First show that first, she's a "people pleaser" and it's excruciatingly difficult for her to risk upsetting someone and therefore not like her if she bluntly states the problem. Explain that people in her past, including her parents and romantic interests, have angrily interpreted this as an accusation or criticism. Second, reveal that people in her past who kindly agreed to comply, never sustained change. Their persistently noisy eating habits made her avoid sharing meals with them or stop dating them altogether. This alerts the reader that, based on past experiences, your character now feels it's pointless to explain this to her dream date.

You can definitely apply this to nonfiction when sharing family stories and business conflicts. Sometimes these internal and external clashes *are* the story. For example, say the book is about two best friends who decide to open a sporting goods business. They are football fanatics who attended rival colleges. At times, they have argued so passionately about games, they feared it would fracture their friendship. Yet they are brilliant in business together.

So, how did they use their football rivalry to their advantage? By branding the business with team rivalry themes, and even hosting game-watching parties and group trips to the Super Bowl. They also offer special game-day deals that engage customers who love or hate certain teams, and they give customers the chance to earn loyalty points and perks for participation. In their book that shares their business success blueprint, the narrative continues to crank up the tension with how the best friends/business partners clash! This could create a high-energy, exciting read that celebrates the company's origin story and endears people—especially sports fans—as loyal customers.

How to Use Multiple Points of View (POV)

This technique is a sophisticated way to add texture to your stories and hook your readers. When you use multiple points of view:

- Chapters alternate between characters;
- Each POV advances the plot or deepens understanding; and
- Multiple points of view enrich the storytelling and heighten drama.

When Elizabeth wrote her first novel entirely from the point of view of her heroine, editor Natalia Aponte at the Tor/Forge imprint of St. Martin's Press said the storytelling felt "claustrophobic." Natalia suggested that Elizabeth revise the manuscript to include chapters from the POV of the villain, the hero, and several other characters. The result was suspense, conflict, and a deeply textured reading experience because the reader gets to "see" the story through the viewpoints of multiple characters who have different and possibly opposing goals.

If you're writing a novel, study your favorites to understand how you can emulate the techniques that make you love them. You can also analyze some of the most popular novels, which include:

Harry Potter and the Sorcerer's Stone by J. K. Rowling

1984 by George Orwell

The Great Gatsby by F. Scott Fitzgerald

The Handmaid's Tale by Margaret Atwood

The Alchemist by Paulo Coelho

Pride and Prejudice by Jane Austen

Moby-Dick by Herman Melville

The Catcher in the Rye by J. D. Salinger

Jane Eyre by Charlotte Brontë

The Lord of the Rings by J. R. R. Tolkien

Little Women by Louisa May Alcott

Beloved by Toni Morrison

To Kill a Mockingbird by Harper Lee

The Hunger Games by Suzanne Collins

Gone Girl by Gillian Flynn

Consider the Elements of Format

Let your personality shine when you design the format of your book. Here's where you can find the sweet spot between a writing style that delights you, and a format that your target readers enjoy most.

When Elizbeth wrote her bestselling memoir, *God's Answer is Know: Lessons From a Spiritual Life,* she created three sections and filled them with vignettes woven around four major themes. She was intuitively guided to use this structure. She trusted the guidance that came from within her—not from whatever was hot on the market. As a result, readers love it.

As a first-time author, you may lack the confidence to trust yourself to make these decisions, but here's your chance to take a risk and really go with the flow of what your heart and soul are directing you to do.

Writing a book is *art*. The greatest artists in history and contemporary times didn't follow what was trending or popular. They unleashed their creative genius to create unique masterpieces that are worth mind-blowing amounts of money and are treasured in museums. Emulate their bold spirits. Playing it safe and following the crowd can be boring and unoriginal. Remember, sometimes the greatest risks lead to the greatest rewards.

So, how do you want to present your content? Consider sections, chapters, sub-topics, and vignettes. Also think about how you can provide visual variety by including:

- Large quotes, facts, or statistics in text boxes.
- Graphics that show data with colorful charts.
- Reflection questions or exercises at the end of each chapter.
- Lines for writing.
- A workbook section at the end of the book.

The purpose of your book will determine whether you include these elements. Will you use it as required reading in your workshops or online courses? Do you want the reader to have a hands-on, interactive experience? Or do you want to provide an uninterrupted reading experience?

Do Your Book, Your Way!

We're presenting these concepts as guides, not rules. Truth be told, you should structure your book based on what you're probably *already using out loud*—in conversations, workshops, podcasts, or talks. Now's the time to tune into that and put it on paper.

As with any book, you cheat yourself out of creating the most impactful and authentic messaging if you try to fit into someone else's structure because you think you "should." Please push cancel-clear-delete on that word. It's stifling! Express yourself *your way!* Think about how you resonate with people in person; that's how you can relate to them on the pages of your book. Figure out what that is, and go for it!

When you master this, you'll write a book that sells, changes lives, and makes you feel proud about what you created and contributed as part of your life's legacy.

OUTLINE YOUR BOOK

On page 90, you'll find a blank outline for a ten-chapter book. You can use it to create your outline.

Begin with a Bang!

The first sentence of your book should bedazzle your readers in a single glance by sparking an emotional response—shock, bliss, trauma, hope—or by offering an unusual twist on something ordinary. Then every sentence after that should continue to hook your readers into a trance-like state where the world around them falls silent and still, and they are wholly consumed by your storytelling, whether fiction or nonfiction.

This "out of body experience" is our barometer for great writing. It happens all the time when we're reading our authors' manuscripts. And you know it's happening when you find yourself swept through a portal into the author's world where the captivating story consumes your focus, engages your senses, and grips your attention.

Even if you're a first-time writer, you *can* craft sentences and scenes that make your reader gasp . . . cause their pulses to race with suspense . . . or make their hearts flutter with excitement.

Simply allow your creative genius to escape the confines of everyday thinking, break free from fear, doubt, and worries about what anyone thinks, and let your wildest, most unbridled ideas splash onto the page. You can do this whether you're writing a novel, a memoir, or a business book. This is what will make your book stand out from the competition, by expressing something unique that people are ready to hear but that no author has yet expressed. Examples include nonfiction books like *The Tipping Point* and *Outliers* by Malcolm Gladwell, and novels like the Harry Potter series by J.K. Rowling, and memoirs such as Brittney Griner's *Coming Home*.

When you sustain this mission to captivate your readers

all the way to the last page, people will tell you:

"The only thing I hated about your book was that it ended."

Or: "I was walking around the office reading your book, and bumping into walls, because I couldn't put it down."

Or: "I was so engaged in your book on the airplane that when we landed, I didn't want to get off because I wanted to keep reading, and the flight attendants had to come and tell me to leave the plane."

These are actual statements that readers shared with Elizabeth about reading her bestselling novel, *Dark Secret*, first published in hardcover in 2000 by the Tor/Forge imprint of St. Martin's Press, then re-released by Two Sisters in 2017.

To capture your reader's attention from the first line of your memoir, take them to a painful, exciting, hilarious, and/or shocking moment to hook them and introduce the book's major premise and promise. Make your readers feel the emotions. Then, sustain the suspense by keeping them on an emotional rollercoaster that jolts their curiosity and teases with cliffhangers at the end of each chapter. A cliffhanger makes your reader feel they are at the edge of a cliff, with no idea how to get back down to flat land. They can only find out by turning the page.

How can you create this rhythm in your book? Elizabeth created the following "how-to memoir" to demonstrate for you.

Write the First Sentence and Opening Scene

Here's an example of a "how-to memoir"—also known as a Hybrid: Life Story + Business Book—that Elizabeth created to demonstrate how to "begin with a bang" on page one. It's titled:

From Wrecked to Wealthy:
How I Built an Empire on the Ashes of my Disastrous Life,
and You Can, Too
By Claudette Caroline Teale

The title reveals the book's promise, and the book cover shows the author wearing a business suit while standing in front of her sleek downtown building emblazoned with a sign that says Queen T Technologies. The book cover also says, "a Fortune 500 company," and that the foreword is written by a prominent business leader whom you admire.

All of this appeals to the author's target audience—people who want to learn how to build a multi-million business, especially if they're starting with nothing, and even moreso if they are beginning amidst trauma and devastating circumstances.

Here's how to start the story. Notice which details pique your interest and keep you reading.

Chapter 1: Wrecked

My stomach cramped as his Ferrari roared into the garage. My phone said 9:09 a.m. While sitting here alone all night in the enormous white-marbled, chandeliered kitchen of our mansion, I checked my phone almost every minute to see if he'd responded to my dozens of texts and calls.

But my husband had been radio silent since the lamb chops had stopped sizzling on the stove and our dinner grew cold on the table.

Why have I believed his lies for so long? Why have I allowed myself to feel trapped and powerless while he controls everything?

Fatigue burned in my eyes. Sadness ached in my heart. And when he finally walked in, his eyes sparkling and his face glowing like he'd just had a ridiculously good time with another woman, I swallowed hard to stop the vomit.

He'd promised to stop. But this was the tenth time.

Before I could say anything, he smiled and said, "We're done. I'm in love with someone else. I want a divorce. Leave now."

Would you keep reading? Why? What emotions does this scene trigger for you?

When writing a scene like this, you'll continue by showing the woman's internal dialogue as she stares at him in disbelief, spiraling into a panic as she thinks about how she'd given everything to their joint business. How she has no money, because it's tied up in the house and the company, how she has no family, and now, how she has no hope.

Continue the chapter with an argument, and conclude with a cliffhanger:

> After he broke my heart, I didn't know where I would go. How I would get there. Or how I would survive. But I had to escape this pain. So, I fled the house in my socks, numb to the shock of snow and ice under my feet, wandering down my street, sobbing so hard that I stumbled into a snowbank. Then everything went black.

Would you turn the page? Remember, the book cover's image and title promise that she becomes very successful in business, and that she's going to teach you how. As a result, you *know* she'll survive and thrive. But how?

Writing Chapter 2

If you begin with a bang and end Chapter 1 on a cliffhanger, your Chapter 2 can provide insight into who you are now—the image of success that your readers want to emulate. That will inspire them to keep reading subsequent chapters that share your blueprint for personal and professional success.

To do this, fast-forward from Chapter 1's cliffhanger to your current state of success. Describe where you are now, and provide some information about how you healed from the "begin with a bang" experience in Chapter 1. Here's an example:

Chapter 2: Wealthy

I'm standing in the soaring, ten-story atrium of the office building that I own, where my 5,000 employees are helping my business achieve record profits. It seems like forever ago since the day my life literally plunged into a snowbank and everything went black. At the time, I had exactly $20 in my pocket.

Since that day when I woke up in the hospital with frostbite, hypothermia, and a broken heart, I've built a business that made $200,000 during the first year and I'm about to hit the $100 million mark.

Now I stand here by the indoor fountain and greet employees every morning at 9:09 a.m., to commemorate that fateful moment when I lost my fairytale dream and gained the grit to become a globally celebrated entrepreneur.

If I can do it, anyone can.

Are you intrigued? This chapter would continue by detailing the glory of her current success, such as being a featured commentator on major television news programs, engaging in philanthropy that helps aspiring entrepreneurs get the funding required to start a new business, and expanding her company's services around the world. Then each chapter would share her step-by-step process for readers to achieve similar success.

How to Outline Your Hybrid: Life Story + Business Book

Now that you've seen how to start the book, follow by presenting one success secret in each chapter to explain how to accomplish the book's promise. For example, an outline could look like this:

Introduction, which includes Your Summary Sentence

Chapter 1 — Begin with a Bang, a shocking crisis scenario

Chapter 2 — My Life Now, success in my most desirable life.

Chapter 3 — Step 1 to Success

Chapter 4 — Step 2 to Success

Chapter 5 — Step 3 to Success

Chapter 6 — Step 4 to Success

Chapter 7 — Step 5 to Success

Chapter 8 — Step 6 to Success

Chapter 9 — Step 7 to Success

Chapter 10 — Step 8 to Success

Chapter 11 — Step 9 to Success

Chapter 12 — Extra wisdom, advice

Resources — Your Bio, contact information, coupons, resources.

How to Embellish the Outline for a Hybrid: Life Story + Business Book

Let's use a chapter *From Wrecked to Wealthy* as an example for how to embellish a chapter. Here's what it might look like:

Chapter 5: Assess Your Skills, Resources, and Mindset

A. Assess your skills & passions to decide on what type of business to create
    i. What do I love to do?
    ii. What are my natural talents?
    iii. How can I make money combining the above?

B. Evaluate your resources to get started
    i. What do I need to start?
    ii. What do I already have?

iii. What person, bank, or agency can help me secure what I need?

C. Psych yourself up!
    i. What am I afraid of? Study how to overcome fear.
    ii. Look at past successes.
    iii. Get a mentor and network with successful entrepreneurs.

Writing and publishing a "how-to memoir" or hybrid memoir/business book is a powerful way to preserve your legacy and share your success blueprint with people who need your guidance.

Outlining Your Memoir

Let's explore how to outline a memoir that simply tells your life story. You can decide if you want a linear chronology or whether you want to hopscotch around the years. If you do that, make sure you use transitions that help your reader follow your jumps through time.

Here's a sample outline.

Introduction, which includes Your Summary Sentence.

Chapter 1 — Begin with a Bang, a shocking crisis scenario or something extraordinary. Introduce themes/issues that you'll weave throughout the tapestry of your life/story/content and that permeate the problem and the solution. Highlight major problems, internal and external.

Chapter 2 — My Life Now, success in my most desirable life.

Chapter 3 — Parents, birth, childhood + context of when/how
I grew up + big dreams.

Chapter 4 — Teen & young adult years.

Chapter 5 — Career dreams + realities.

Chapter 6 — Love, marriage, family.

Chapter 7 — Travel. Illness. Family crisis. Career change.
Turmoil, upheaval.

Chapter 8 — Major crisis where internal & external problems
combust.

Chapter 9 — How I resolved the crisis, healed, and rose from
the ashes.

Chapter 10 — What the future holds.

Resources — Your Bio, contact information, resources.

How to Embellish the Outline for Your Memoir

Here's an example for a memoir with continuous storytelling.

Chapter 3 — Parents, Birth, Childhood. Establish themes.

A. Parents
  i. Their family histories provide context for your life.
  ii. Mom
  iii. Dad
  iv. Marriage, family, conflicts, divorce, death,
      unconventional things.

B. Birth
  i. Details including family dynamics + historical
      events.
  ii. Framing in mentality & conventions of the time.
  iii. Events that highlight the major themes of your life.

C. Childhood

     i. Happy times. Favorite fun. Biggest fears.
         Traumatic events.
    ii. School. Good, bad, details!
   iii. Biggest dreams.

Expand your outline with at least three stories or topics for each chapter. Bolster your points with information such as anecdotes, statistics, graphics, photographs, quotes, diagrams, and other material that enhances your stories.

In your book, which story best enables you to **begin with a bang?**

_____

_____

_____

_____

Make Timelines!

Creating a timeline is an excellent way to organize your material and construct the chronology of your life, your family's history, your business, and your main characters in a novel. You can also use timelines to help you mentally organize a particular experience, such as a relationship, your education, or a marriage.

You can create your timeline(s) on a spreadsheet with multiple tabs for each person, character, or experience. You can type a timeline in a Microsoft Word document. In the first column or on the left side of the page, list the years. If you're writing your life story, start with your birthday. Or if you're including your family's history, and you've researched your family tree back to 1385 in France, for example, start there.

Then list the years where something important happened, such as the dates when your family immigrated to Canada as fur traders, then to Michigan as loggers, which led you to open a famous bed & breakfast in your family's centuries-old log cabin, and now your book aims to promote your business.

The possibilities are endless, but let's keep it simple.

Beside each year, briefly describe a formative moment or experience that relates to the themes that you're highlighting. It's helpful to reference the list of themes that you created on page 54, and use those as threads on which you'll weave the texture of your stories and the entire book. In your spreadsheet, you can create columns for "themes" and check off which apply to each milestone or experience.

Remember that no story—fiction or nonfiction—takes place in a vacuum. Current events were, and always are, happening. Use them to provide context for your story. For example, you wouldn't write that your characters enjoyed a wonderful honeymoon in Hawaii on December 7, 1941. That's the day that the Japanese bombed Pearl Harbor, killing more than 2,400 Americans and inciting the United States to declare war on Japan. How do you prevent historical *faux pas* like this? Go to Wikipedia and enter a specific year; it will list major news events and pop culture information from that year.

You can make your timeline as stark or as detailed as you'd like. It's not required, but it's *very* helpful. As an example, here's a portion of the timeline that Elizabeth created while writing her memoir around themes of race/religion, food/fat, fear, and divorce/healing/harmony:

1967—Born to interracial couple who sparked racial & religious scandal. Father disowned by family; parents excommunicated by Catholic church. U.S. Supreme Court ruling *Loving v. Virginia* strikes down laws in 16 states banning interracial marriage. Detroit insurrection & other riots. Hippie Summer of Love in San Francisco. Baptism, Princess of Peace. Race & religion themes.

1968—Climbed onto grandmother's lap, broke the ice to heal family rift resulting in harmony and love. Race theme. Sister Catherine is born. Dr. King was assassinated.

1969—Vietnam War + protests.

1970—Loved to eat. Food & fat theme.

1971

1972—Molested by neighbor. Terrified entire childhood. Fear theme.

1973—Cousin called me Fatso. Mother started dieting. Self-consciousness begins. Food & fat theme.

1974—Moved from Black/Mexican neighborhood in Saginaw, Michigan, to mostly Jewish and diverse Oak Park, a Detroit suburb.

1975—Mixed-race girl, questions, never fitting in. Race/identity theme.

1976—Oakland County Child Killer. Fear theme. America's bicentennial.

1977—Read *The Exorcist* & *Amityville Horror*. Fear theme.

1978—Middle school, never fitting in. Skinny girls w/straight hair. Started extreme dieting at age 11. Dramatic cycles of weight gain and loss. Race/identity, food, fat.

1979

1980—Left multicultural Oak Park for homogenous, affluent Okemos. Race/identity, food, fat.

Elizabeth creates similar timelines for characters in her fiction novels.

Whether you're writing nonfiction or fiction, these timelines will help you mentally and visually organize your material.

Understanding Front Matter and Back Matter

You're going to sandwich the delicious substance of your book between its front matter and its back matter. Your publisher may insert some of this material for you. Make sure to ask what parts you need to compose and/or compile and share with your publisher, preferably in the first draft of your manuscript. You'll definitely need to provide the dedication, acknowledgements, introduction, preface, prologue, information for end notes and/or footnotes, references, a bibliography, and your author bio. If you're self-publishing, you'll need to compile this information yourself and stack it into the book in the correct order according to publishing industry standards.

Here follow lists of **standard front and back matter elements** with **brief definitions that adhere to the guidelines of** *The Chicago Manual of Style*. They are in the order that they should appear in your book. Please note that front matter and back matter differ for memoirs, business books, and novels.

The Front Matter of Your Book

1. **The Title Page** displays the full book title, subtitle, author name, and publisher. This is your book's official identification page.

2. **The Copyright Page** contains legal and publishing information, including:

- Copyright notice
- ISBN
- Publisher
- Edition information
- Rights statements
- Disclaimer (if applicable)
- Credits for author photos

3. **The Dedication** is a short personal message where you dedicate the book to a person or group. This is optional and adds a nice touch.

4. The Epigraph is a quote, poem, or passage that sets the tone or theme of the book. It's usually placed before the main text begins. This is optional.

5. The Table of Contents lists chapters (and sometimes sections) with page numbers. It helps readers navigate the book. Page numbers are added after the graphic designer formats the interior; any page numbers that you list on your manuscript will not be the same in your published book, so don't waste time adding them yourself.

6. The Foreword is a short introductory piece composed by a celebrity, leader, expert, public figure, or prominent person who endorses the book, elevates credibility, and tells readers why the book matters and why they should read it. This is optional. Cedric King's book has two Forewords, one by Starbucks Chairman Emeritus Howard Schultz and the other by actor Gary Sinise, founder of The Gary Sinise Foundation that helps wounded veterans.

7. The Preface is composed by you to explain why you wrote the book, how it was conceived, or how to read it. This is optional.

8. The Acknowledgments are where you can thank people and/or organizations that helped you achieve the goal of writing, publishing, and promoting your book. You can thank one person or everyone back to your third-grade teacher who inspired you. This is optional. Sometimes authors insert these at the end of the book. Our authors usually thank us here and we immensely appreciate that.

9. The Introduction is your welcome note to your readers to introduce them to the subject, purpose, and structure of your book. It prepares the them for what's coming without revealing the main content. Here's where you can weave in your Summary Sentence to tell your readers why you wrote the book and how this book can help them.

Sometimes novels and memoirs start with a **Prologue**, which is a brief scene that usually occurs before the main story or content begin. A prologue should be intriguing as it reveals a dramatic moment, background information, and context that all ignite the reader's curiosity and establish the tone for the remainder of the book.

After you've placed the relevant Front Matter in your manuscript, your book actually begins with Chapter One.

Remember:

You have the creative authority to select which of these to include in your book. Consider:

- **Memoirs** often include a dedication, acknowledgments, and an introduction.
- **Business books** usually include a foreword and introduction.
- **Novels** often have minimal front matter.

Two Sisters places testimonial quotes on the very first pages of the book under the heading, "What People Are Saying About [AUTHOR'S NAME]." This comes before the title page. These quotes that the author solicits from people who know and respect them are important because:

1) They provide the reader with personal or professional insights about the author, boosting their social credibility; and

2) Each person who provides a quote will serve as an ambassador to tell others about the book because they are proud to be included in it.

The Back Matter of Your Book

Back matter is the content at the end of your book. Here's a clear, publishing industry-standard list of Back Matter, with a brief definition of each. This works well for memoirs, business books, and novels (with a few optional items depending on your genre).

Acknowledgements. In this section, you can express gratitude to loved ones, friends, mentors, editors, your publisher, your literary agent, and supporters who helped make your book a reality. This is often in the Front Matter.

About the Author. Here's where you can tell readers about yourself, by providing **a** short biography. It establishes your credibility, shares your education and background, and reveals your connection to the topics in your book. You can include your official author photo as well as contact information such as a website, your social media handles, and even a phone number, email address, and physical address if you're publishing a business book and have a brick-and-mortar store.

Author's Note. Here's where you can include reflections or clarifications that didn't fit into the main narrative. This is common in memoirs and historical works.

Afterword. In this reflective closing section, you can share your final thoughts, lessons learned, or updates since the story ended.

Appendix (or Appendices). This contains supplemental material that supports the book, including worksheets, tools, timelines, documents, exercises, and explanations.

Footnotes / Endnotes. These include citations, references, or explanations related to specific passages in the book, and are often used in nonfiction, memoirs, and research-based works. Two Sisters uses Endnotes with a superscript number in the text and the actual citation at the end of the book. Sometimes footnotes, which are indicated by a superscript number and appear at the bottom of that same page, are appropriate when you want your reader to understand a point or see the source without needing to turn to the back of the book.

Bibliography / References. This is a list of books, articles, interviews, and sources that you consulted or referenced while writing the book.

Resources. These are books, websites, organizations, hotlines, or tools that you recommend for readers who want more information about your subject.

Discussion Questions / Book Club Guide. You can include these questions to inspire reflection and conversation. They're helpful in book clubs, classrooms, retreats, and workshops.

Call to Action. Here's your chance to invite readers to take the next step—visit your website, join your community, attend events, register for your class or retreat, participate in your fan club, invite you to speak, and connect on social media. You could also include a coupon to attract customers to your business.

Inside his book, *Confessions of a Plastic Surgeon,* Dr. Jeneby includes a coupon for services at his spa and surgery center in San Antonio, Texas. One page says, "A Gift for You. As a THANK YOU for purchasing this book, I'd like to offer you a special discount. Bring your book to your appointment, and you'll receive an instant discount." The coupon promises larger discounts for those who purchase the hardcover version of his book.

Index. This is an alphabetical list of topics and names with page numbers to help readers quickly find information. This is optional and is more commonly found in nonfiction books. We created an index for *Let the Future Begin* by Dennis W. Archer. If you choose to make an index, wait until your book is formatted by the graphic designer because the page numbers on your manuscript will be different in the published book.

Permissions / Credits *(if needed)*. Here you can acknowledge copyrighted material that you're reprinting with permission, such as song lyrics, poems, or excerpts from published books.

Remember:

Back matter is prime real estate for:

- Inviting readers into your world.
- Expanding your email list.
- Promoting yourself for speaking engagements.

Think of it as a strategic extension of your book.

Breathe Life into Your Book

Think of yourself as breathing life into an idea that becomes a living document—your book. This worksheet can help you gain clarity as you prepare to write your book.

Your Book Title:_____

Identity: Write your Summary Sentence.

_____

_____

_____

_____

Skeleton: Write the major points that you want to share. For example, "8 Steps to Create & Sustain a Healthy Lifestyle" with a heading for each specific step.

_____

_____

_____

_____

Many aspiring authors say, "I don't know where to start or what to include!" So, here's an easy and effective way to jumpstart your flow of ideas.

First, make a list of your favorite stories that you're always telling about your life or your business, along with stories that people are always telling about you. At dinner parties, holiday gatherings, weddings—what are those hilarious, poignant, inspiring, tragic, enraging—you pick the emotion—stories that you're known for? These *must* go into your book.

If you're writing a memoir, these are stories from your life that pertain to the themes you're highlighting in your book. If you're composing a business book, these are stories relating to how you started your company, so tie them to lessons learned and instruction you're sharing as your success blueprint. If you're writing a novel, you may have envisioned specific scenes that form the tentpoles of your story, so start by listing those scenes, then flesh them out.

Story #1_____.

Story #2_____.

Story #3_____.

Story #4_____.

Story #5_____.

Story #6_____.

Story #7_____.

Story #8_____.

Story #9_____.

Story #10_____.

Heartbeat: As the author of this book, your promise to the reader is to help them solve a problem. What problem is your book going to solve for the reader?

_____

_____

_____

_____

Authority: Explain what makes you an authority on this topic and why the reader should trust the information and solutions you're offering to solve their problem.

_____

_____

_____

_____

Point of View (POV): Describe your "voice" as you're speaking to your target audience. Is it conversational, formal, humorous? It should be authentic to you while appropriate for and appealing to your target audience.

_____

_____

_____

_____

Appearance: Describe your writing style, book cover, book design, photos, graphics, quotes, hardcover/paperback/eBook, etc. Is it a coffee table book? A pocket-sized daily motivational? Do you want black and white interior or color?

_____

_____

_____

_____

Flesh It Out: Continue to flesh out each point.

_____

_____

_____

_____

Perform Literary Liposuction: Trim the flab with editing. We'll do this later!

Let's Outline Your Book

      TITLE_____

      BY_____

1. CHAPTER 1. TITLE: _____

Begin with a bang—a story that is shocking, unusual, traumatic, triumphant, and will grab your reader's attention and keep it.

_____

_____

_____

_____

      A. Heading 1_____

            i. _____

            ii. _____

            iii. _____

      B. Heading 2_____

            i. _____

            ii. _____

            iii. _____

      C. Heading 3_____

            i. _____

            ii. _____

            iii. _____

2. CHAPTER 2. TITLE: _____

Tell a story that introduces and illustrates the topic of this chapter.

_____

_____

_____

    A. Heading 1_____

        i. _____

        ii. _____

        iii. _____

    B. Heading 2_____

        i. _____

        ii. _____

        iii. _____

    C. Heading 3_____

        i. _____

        ii. _____

        iii. _____

3. CHAPTER 3. TITLE: _____

Tell a story that introduces and illustrates the topic of this chapter.

_____

_____

_____

A. Heading 1_____

    i. _____

    ii. _____

    iii. _____

B. Heading 2_____

    i. _____

    ii. _____

    iii. _____

C. Heading 3_____

    i. _____

    ii. _____

    iii. _____

4. CHAPTER 4. TITLE: _____

Tell a story that introduces and illustrates the topic of this chapter.

_____

_____

_____

A. Heading 1_____

    i. _____

    ii. _____

    iii. _____

B. Heading 2_____

    i. _____

      ii. _____

      iii. _____

  C. Heading 3_____

      i. _____

      ii. _____

      iii. _____

5. CHAPTER 5. TITLE: _____

Tell a story that introduces and illustrates the topic of this chapter.

_____

_____

_____

  A. Heading 1_____

      i. _____

      ii. _____

      iii. _____

  B. Heading 2_____

      i. _____

      ii. _____

      iii. _____

  C. Heading 3_____

      i. _____

      ii. _____

      iii. _____

6. CHAPTER 6. TITLE: _____

Tell a story that introduces and illustrates the topic of this chapter.

_____

_____

_____

    A. Heading 1_____

        i. _____

        ii. _____

        iii. _____

    B. Heading 2_____

        i. _____

        ii. _____

        iii. _____

    C. Heading 3_____

        i. _____

        ii. _____

        iii. _____

7. CHAPTER 7. TITLE: _____

Tell a story that introduces and illustrates the topic of this chapter.

_____

_____

_____

    A. Heading 1_____

        i. _____

  ii. _____

  iii. _____

B. Heading 2_____

  i. _____

  ii. _____

  iii. _____

C. Heading 3_____

  i. _____

  ii. _____

  iii. _____

8. CHAPTER 8. TITLE: _____

Tell a story that introduces and illustrates the topic of this chapter.

_____

_____

_____

A. Heading 1_____

  i. _____

  ii. _____

  iii. _____

B. Heading 2_____

  i. _____

  ii. _____

  iii. _____

C. Heading 3_____

      i. _____

      ii. _____

      iii. _____

9. CHAPTER 9. TITLE: _____

Tell a story that introduces and illustrates the topic of this chapter.

_____

_____

_____

   A. Heading 1_____

      i. _____

      ii. _____

      iii. _____

   B. Heading 2_____

      i. _____

      ii. _____

      iii. _____

   C. Heading 3_____

      i. _____

      ii. _____

      iii. _____

10. CHAPTER 10. TITLE: _____

Tell a story that introduces and illustrates the topic of this chapter.

_____

_____

_____

    A. Heading 1_____

        i. _____

        ii. _____

        iii. _____

    B. Heading 2_____

        i. _____

        ii. _____

        iii. _____

    C. Heading 3_____

        i. _____

        ii. _____

        iii. _____

SECTION 3

MASTER THE MECHANICS OF WRITING & STORYTELLING

It's time to learn writing secrets that engage your reader: Your book will be competing with the multimedia extravaganza of our digital world, so here you'll learn techniques that make your words jump up off the page and dance for your readers . . . keeping them hooked from page one until the last word. Their only complaint about your book will be that *it ended*. Then they'll tell everyone they know that they *must* read your book.

WHAT IS GREAT WRITING?

*"Writing is a divine art, and the more I write and read, the more
I love it."*
— Virginia Woolf

- Think of your favorite books. What makes you love them? The style, the message, the topic, the feelings that they evoke in you?
- Great writing sweeps you into your imagination and keeps you there.
- It is clear, concise, and conversational.
- It appeals to your emotions and inspires you to take action.
- Memorable writing comes from deep within you and speaks from your soul.
- It happens when you immerse into your creative flow.

You capture and keep people's attention with intriguing stories. Whether you're writing fiction or nonfiction, you need to strengthen and flex your storytelling skills. And if you're writing a nonfiction family history with scant details, then your storytelling skills will help you preserve oral histories. So, let's explore how to improve your writing skills and use techniques to hook your reader from the first line to the end.

Make Your Readers Experience the Scene with All Six Senses
The best stories make you feel like you're *inside* each scene, with all your senses engaged. This cultivates an emotional connection to the storytelling, and that compels you to keep reading. So, your job as an author is to make your readers

experience the story by engaging their six senses: **sight, hearing, touch taste, smell, and intuition**.

For example, if a scene takes place in a nice restaurant, don't simply say that the people/characters are having dinner and that the food is good. Invite the reader to hear the garlic butter sizzling on a cast-iron platter as the server sets a ribeye steak on the white linen-covered table. Let them inhale the rich aroma and take in the sight of a perfectly-cooked entrée.

Describe the weight of the fork and knife in the hand. With the first bite, allow the reader to savor the flavor and tenderness. Layer in sound—the soft tinkle of live piano music, the clink of silverware against china, the low murmur of conversation in the room.

Ground the scene in touch and atmosphere: the velvet chair beneath them, the plush décor, the chandelier sparkling overhead. Finally, bring in emotion. Perhaps there's a glass of exceptional Cabernet Sauvignon on the table and, across the candlelit glow, someone who makes the heart flutter—gazing at you as if you're the only person on the planet.

Don't you feel *that?* When you write this way, your reader isn't observing the scene. **They're living it.** And so are you, which makes it more fun as the writer.

Keep in mind that you can heighten the reader's emotional response when you select words that convey the vibe of the scene. So, for example, in the fancy restaurant scene above, rather than playing up the luxe ambiance, you could say that the scent of garlic is so strong, it makes the character feel nauseous. The piano player is crooning their wedding dance song, which leaves a sour taste in your character's mouth because he just went through a hostile break-up and was hoping this date would make him believe in love again.

Here's a sample scene that Elizabeth composed to illustrate this concept. As you read, identify the six senses.

The screeching coffee machines punctuated the

tense silence between Alicia and her boyfriend. Tears welled in his eyes, then dripped down his red cheeks. She held her breath to stop inhaling the scent of coffee, which had been delicious upon entering this café but was now as bitter as the cold love hanging like icicles between them. The bustle of people around them—chatting, typing on laptops, and sipping expensive drinks—faded to silent black and white stillness. She wanted to scream and smile all at once. But no words would come from her sour mouth. Because the irony of the moment as he broke her heart and freed her spirit all at once, was paralyzing her with shock.

Now it's your turn. Take five minutes to write or rewrite a scene from your book by using your six senses. If you don't have a scene written, then please compose one here.

Sight * Hearing * Touch * Taste * Smell * Gut Feeling/Intuition

_____

_____

_____

_____

_____

_____

_____

_____

Show, Don't Tell
Avoid Verbs Like Hear, See, Smell, Taste, Touch, Feel

It's not wrong to "tell" a story. However, when you "show" what's happening through the eyes of each character in a novel or person in a memoir or business book, the writing is more energetic and impactful.

Therefore, when writing to engage your reader's senses, describe their experience **without** using the words see, hear, touch, taste, smell, or feel intuitively. Show it. You'll see that the storytelling flows more smoothly when clunky and unnecessary words are removed. Likewise, less is more. You want to pack the most powerful punch with as few words as possible. This word economy energizes your writing and hooks your reader. Here's an example.

First draft, telling: While Sally napped on her patio, *she was annoyed that she could hear the sound* of the train whistle blowing while its mighty weight *made a deep rumbling noise* on the rickety tracks and *could be heard*, jolting her out of her sleep. *43 words*

Revised, showing: While Sally napped on her patio, the passing train's *shrill whistle and deep rumbling* on the rickety tracks jolted her awake and she *scowled. 24 words*

Let's break this down. First, notice how we "show" that she was annoyed by writing that she "scowled." Second, we removed "hear the sound" with "shrill whistle and deep rumbling." Those *are* sounds. Third, we removed "could be heard," because it's obvious that Sally was hearing the noise. Notice that every sentence does not have to include all six senses.

Do you see how this packs a more powerful punch with more concise and energetic writing?

Use Actions to Show, Not Tell

Don't just describe. Show with actions.

Telling: *He loved her and didn't want her to be cold.*
Showing: *He removed his suit jacket and gently draped it over her bare shoulders.*

His action of removing his jacket—risking his own exposure to the chilly air—shows that he's putting her comfort first, and his gentle draping illustrates his love and concern for her comfort.

Now it's your turn. Rewrite the sentence to show her emotion.

Telling: *She was sad and was crying loudly and shaking.*
Showing:

_____

_____

Use Active Verbs and Avoid Passive Verbs

Passive verbs are not wrong. They're just boring! They are clunky and indicate that you need to replace them a high-energy, interesting verb to jazz up the writing.

Active verbs show the subject of the sentence *doing* something, while **passive verbs** show something *being done to* the subject while weakening the action and impact.

Passive: The book *was published by* the business owner.

Active: The business owner *published* the book.

Passive: Her outfit *was accented by* a red scarf.

Active: A red scarf *accented* her outfit.

Or: A red scarf *jazzed up* her outfit.

Watch out for passive verbs phrases such as "could be seen" and "there were" or "there was."

Passive: *There were* fifty-five people in the crowded gallery.

Active: Fifty-five people *packed* the gallery.

Passive: *There was* an obstacle blocking him from attending the concert.

Active: An obstacle *blocked* him from attending the concert.

Why is it important to energize your writing with action verbs? Because, as we've said, you're competing with the sensory extravaganza of our digital world that makes it easier to scroll and *watch* than to focus on the flat pages of a book that require mental effort. So you want to make the reading experience as textured and energized and unique as possible. Action is the answer. Specifically, action verbs. They make your sentences more vivid, clear, and dynamic, so readers *see and feel* what's happening. All while you engage their emotions and accelerate your narrative.

How to Describe People and Places

Have you ever read a book—fiction or nonfiction—where you can't envision the people or the places because the author did not describe them? Our minds crave details, and it's your job to provide them, so readers have a clear mental picture.

Let's use people and places from the 2014 novel, *Husbands, Incorporated*—written by Elizabeth under her *nom de plume*, Sasha Maxwell—to illustrate how you can craft descriptions that reveal important information. Here are several examples.

The main character's 70-year-old parents

Dad's combed-back, silver-black waves framed a sun-weathered face that testified to their years of walking, cycling and golfing. Mom wore her butterscotch-hued hair in a modern bouffant: brushed back, slightly teased on top for volume, then swooping forward in two curls just below her ears. The deep contentment and *joie de vivre* dancing in their blue eyes, and the quickness of their mouths to smile, magnified their resemblance.

Dad's silk tie and dark suit complemented Mom's magenta dress with braided gold trim. They wore diamond wedding bands that they had exchanged during a recent ceremony to renew their vows on their fiftieth wedding anniversary; a new emerald-cut solitaire set in diamond baguettes glistened on Mom's finger.

Note how you can clearly envision this couple *and* you have insight into their lifestyle and happiness.

Business owner Venus Roman

Venus Roman's white suit jacket flared over her slim hips and tapered into a tiny waist adorned with a rhinestone clasp. Her long, toned legs were bare under the slim-fitting skirt. Diamonds sparkled in her ears, and her short blond hair made her look bold. Topping the super glamorous look were silver sunglasses and matching stiletto sandals.

While this describes Venus' appearance, subsequent passages emphasize the "fire" in her eyes, which another character named Jane first notices:

Her eyes glowed with the kind of passion and purpose that Jane viewed as the pinnacle of female power.

Venus' business partner: Raye Johnson

Her almond-shaped brown eyes were ringed with Cleopatra-style black liner, while fire engine red lipstick showcased her full lips and straight, bright-white teeth, thanks to the braces that Raye's ex-husband had insisted that she get. Her radiant, cinnamon-hued skin always looked perfect. With foundation, powder and impeccably arched and waxed eyebrows, her face looked almost air brushed.

But the intelligence and zest for life sparkling like diamonds in her eyes left no doubt; Raye Johnson was far more than just a pretty face.

Her custom-designed, red pin-striped business suit hugged her curves that she kept slim and firm with running, strength-training and yoga.

We just learned that Raye styles herself after an Egyptian queen, that her ex-husband was controlling, and that she's a *boss.*

The hero: Rex Lancaster

His hair, falling in wavy tumbles over his shoulders, was like a lion's mane around his smooth, clean-shaven face. Venus stared up into his large, honey-hued eyes that were framed by perfectly arched, brown brows. His Roman warrior nose was in perfect proportion to his wide jaw and chiseled cheeks. His full lips looked as succulent as fresh raspberries. Tiny silver hoop earrings adorned each ear. His thick neck suggested athletic brawn, and a muscular build filled out the black velvet tuxedo jacket over a stiff, open-collared white shirt and black slacks. His butter-soft, black leather loafers suggested a preference for simplicity, comfort and luxury.

You don't have to get *this* detailed when describing people in your book, however, this example paints a very clear visual of Rex.

<u>A villain</u>

Everything about him exuded a bullish air. He was tall with a thick upper body, and his posture leaned forward, with his wide forehead down, as if he were about to charge and gore any obstacle in his way.

These two sentences let you know that this guy's posture shouts *bully.*

<u>Raye's condo entrance hall</u>

Sultry jazz soothed her mind and muscles as it pulsed through the foyer—a 20-foot, gold marble octagon lit by Egyptian-style sconces. Occupying the wall facing the elevator were two life-sized, black panther statues that appeared to prowl toward each other, their eyes glistening with faux emeralds.

Above them hung a gilt-framed portrait of the legendary Queen of the Nile, and between them was a gold table displaying a crystal vase with two-dozen red roses.

Raye's home décor reflects her personality and her opulent lifestyle, which indicate her wealth status thanks to her business success.

Crank Up the Conflict!

Elizabeth's first editor, Natalia Aponte at the Tor/Forge imprint of St. Martin's Press, which published her first three bestselling romantic thrillers, wisely said:

"Conflict is the engine that drives your story."

Think about a movie. If the hero or heroine conquers the villain in the first scene, the story lacks conflict. The best movies crank up the conflict until the climax, which is the chase, the fight, the explosion, or the confrontation, that hopefully lead to the hero or heroine's victory.

In a soap opera, if everyone is getting along, being honest, staying faithful to their spouses, and honoring friendships, the lack of drama will bore viewers, who will tune out.

Here's a sure-fire secret to crank up the conflict: The closer a person's relationship is with the villain, the more devastation their actions will trigger. For example, if Shirley has an affair with another man, her husband will be furious and sad. If Shirley has an affair with her husband's beloved twin brother, her husband will feel doubly devastated, because his wife cheated on him *and* his brother betrayed him in the worst way.

This concept applies whether you're writing fiction or nonfiction. Whatever you write involves people and storytelling, and the best stories contain conflict and drama that engage your reader's emotions.

Dissect the Anatomy of a Gripping Scene

Natalia also told Elizabeth to read a book that forever changed how she writes. It's called *Scene & Structure* by Jack M. Bickham. This book explains how to create effective scenes—for fiction and nonfiction—that are driven by the following six words:

GOAL:

CONFLICT:

DISASTER:

EMOTION:

DECISION:

ACTION:

These words form the framework for the best scenes. The sequence heightens suspense by structuring each scene around a character's unmet goal that collides with escalating obstacles and culminates in a disaster that triggers emotion, decision, and action, propelling the story forward. Plus, it's fun to craft your scenes this way.

Here's an example that Elizabeth composed to illustrate how this structure creates a suspenseful rhythm.

All Adrienne wants to do right now is write a great opening scene for her book. She finally has a free afternoon alone in the house to focus, get this done, and send it to her editor today.

The rain tapping on the window and the whooshing wind make this the perfect time to stay in and write. *Finally!* With her fingers poised over the keyboard, and her brain revved with coffee, she lets her imagination run wild—

Oh darn, I forgot to buy eggs! I really need to clean the bathroom. What dress am I wearing to the banquet tonight? I hope they serve chocolate cake.

The cursor glows on the blank screen.

"Adrienne, concentrate!" she says out loud. "Focus!"

She starts to type: *The woman's gray pallor and piercing eyes made the hairs on the back of my neck stand up. This woman was evil. And I couldn't escape her—*

Crash!

Adrienne gasps as glass shatters and something *thumps* at the front of the house.

"What???!!!"

She leaps up from her chair and runs into the living room.

A giant tree limb rests on the sofa. Rain is beating down through the broken window; the wind whips the torn curtains.

Terror rips through her. She listens for sirens. *Is this a tornado?* She freezes, paralyzed with fear, wondering what to do next.

She calls her city hall to request a repair crew, then finds a board to cover the broken window to keep the rain out.

And while she waits for the repair crew, she returns to her desk to write. Hopefully.

Now let's dissect the six elements that form the framework for the scene.

GOAL: Adrienne wants to write a great scene and send her manuscript to her editor today.

CONFLICT: She can't concentrate and is not writing.

DISASTER: A tree crashes in the living room. Now she really can't write because she has to clean up, call a repair crew, await their arrival, and oversee their work.

EMOTION: Terror and confusion.

DECISION: Deal with it.

ACTION: Call for help and get back to writing.

Writing exercise: Take five to ten minutes to write or rewrite a scene from your book using this six-part structure:

GOAL: _____

CONFLICT: _____

DISASTER: _____

EMOTION: _____

DECISION: _____

ACTION: _____

This exercise is inspired by the scene-structuring principles that Jack M. Bickham teaches in his book, Scene & Structure *(Writer's Digest Books).*

While you're writing your book, list these six words at the top of every scene, fill in the answers, then compose the most suspenseful experiences for the people in your book.

Find Your Unique Voice

Our author Michal Smith mastered the art of writing from her unique voice in her 2022 coming-of-age book, *The Smell of Lilacs: A Memoir.* Her writing style is poetic and absolutely delightful to read as she chronicles her childhood with her family during the 1950s in the mid-Michigan factory town of Saginaw.

Your "voice" is what makes your book special and authentic. Readers want narrative that sounds like *you.* So here are tips to find your unique voice.

1. Talk to yourself out loud as you write. That way, you can hear exactly how you express yourself without sounding too formal or stiff, which can be a problem for first-time writers. You can also talk to a person who is a willing participant in this exercise and record the conversation with voice-to-text, to capture the exact words and ways that you express yourself.

2. Let your personality shine! Now's your time to express your most authentic self. Not as you think an author "should" sound, and not in the style that other writers use to compose books. This is all about *you*. So think about the unique phrases that you use every day when you're happy or sad or angry.

Here are examples:

-   Do you cuss? Is that appropriate for your book? Several major bestselling books have an F-bomb in the *title*. So, reflect on your Summary Sentence to determine whether to keep your language raw and real—or not.

-   Do you sprinkle "like" or "Oh, man!" throughout your sentences? Our author Joanie Lindenmeyer exclaims "Wowzer!" and "Oh, golly!" and many other words that she included in her books, because that's how she really talks; this makes her personality sparkle on the pages.

-   Perhaps you exclaim phrases in a way that shortens them. For example, some people say, "Oh Lord, have mercy!" and it sounds like, "Oh Lord, *hammercy!*" This adds personality and authenticity to your writing. The first time that this appears in the book, explain this to your reader so they understand your unique abbreviation.

- Do you speak in short, simple sentences? Or are you verbose? Do you use big words? Slang?

- Another tip is to read your writing out loud. Does it sound like you?

Use Authentic Dialogue

When you're composing a memoir or business book and you're quoting other people, make sure that you capture their dialogue exactly as they speak. This is easy if you're interviewing people and recording audio that can be transcribed. Then you simply extract their exact words. However, if you're writing from memory, write dialogue exactly as it was spoken. For example, if you're remembering something your grandfather once told you, recreate the quote with his exact words, and indicate if he spoke with an accent or colloquialisms.

A colloquialism is a word or phrase that people use in everyday, informal conversation such as "yawl" or "y'all," and can reflect a person's origin.

Likewise, most people do not enunciate every syllable. So instead of "I'm going to the store," we might say, "I'm gonna go shopping" or "I'm fixin' to go shopping." Don't be afraid to write dialogue this way; it's authentic. Stiff, formal language feels fake and unrealistic. Plus, it can make every person sound alike.

Another way to enhance the authentic sound of each person's voice is to use dialect. A dialect is a way of speaking that reveals a person's culture or geographic origin where people pronounce words differently and use unique expressions.

Harlem Renaissance superstar Zora Neale Hurston mastered this in her short stories and novels when composing conversations between Southern Black people.

Research & Understand Your Genre

Before you can truly bring your story to life on the page, it's important to pause and get to know the world that your book is entering. Every genre has its own rhythm, expectations, and unspoken "rules" that help readers instantly feel at home in your story. Taking time to research and understand your genre does not limit your creativity; this process empowers it. When you know what readers of your genre love, expect, and are already buying, you can shape your book in a way that feels familiar, satisfying, and irresistible, while staying completely true to your unique voice and message. Here are some tips:

- Know your readers: what they want, what they expect.

- Read bestsellers in your genre.

- Read the online comments under bestsellers to learn what readers love and dislike.

- Research and follow what's hot in the market.

- Pay attention to future trends for books like yours.

- Learn which publishing houses and their imprints publish your genre.

- Explore which literary agents represent your genre.

- Join a writing group or organization that focuses on the type of book you're writing.

- Attend workshops and conferences.

- Understand size: page count and word count. If you aimed to write a certain number of pages or to hit a certain word count, are you within range? Your page count and word count can affect your book in many ways.

- Does your genre require a certain word count?

- Does your publisher's imprint have specific guidelines?

- The page count will determine the manufacturing cost of your book.

- The manufacturing cost will affect the retail price.

The more you understand about your genre from the very beginning, the more smoothly your writing journey will unfold. Knowing who your readers are, what they're looking for, and how books like yours are positioned in the marketplace helps you make confident choices about your content, tone, structure, and even your title. Instead of guessing, you're creating with clarity—and that leads to better books, happier readers, and greater success. Remember, when you start informed, you finish empowered.

Your Journal is a Treasure Trove of Stories for Your Book

Your journal is a treasure trove of stories for your future book—and the sooner you start, the richer it becomes. When you write in your journal in real time, you're capturing your raw, honest feelings in the moment, not the polished or fuzzy version you remember later. You're preserving the sights, sounds, emotions, and tiny details that would otherwise fade with time. So whether you write your book one year from now, ten years from now, or even fifty years from today, you'll have your life beautifully documented—scene by scene. If you've ever thought, *"One day I'll write my book,"* this is your gentle nudge to start now. Your future book is already being written—one journal entry at a time.

Many of our authors have mined their journals for passages that they included in their books.

Among them: Aimee Mackovic, who invites readers into her incredible true story in *Contains Recycled Parts: My Triple Organ Transplant Journey and the Science of Gratitude*, which we were honored to publish in 2023. With warmth, humor, and an open heart, Aimee shares what it was like to survive not one, but *three* life-saving transplants—heart, liver, and kidney—while choosing gratitude, resilience, and hope every step of the way. Through journal entries, Facebook posts, and real-time reflections, she weaves together the science of medicine with the love of family, friends, donors, and donor families, creating a moving and uplifting story that proves it's possible to survive life's most frightening moments, then truly thrive.

Like many of our books, Aimee's memoir is a helpful companion for anyone navigating a health crisis—and for anyone who loves an engaging, heartfelt read that will make you laugh, cry, and cherish life with deeper optimism, love, and gratitude.

SECTION 4

EDITING

It's time to trim the flab! We call this "literary liposuction." Every first draft has flubbery sentences and sections, redundancies, tangents, repetition, and extraneous information. We'll show you fun ways to identify what to extract during the editing process, so that every word propels your narrative with power and purpose.

LET'S SHAPE YOUR MANUSCRIPT INTO A STRONG, LEAN MASTERPIECE

You wrote your first draft. Now it's time to tone and trim it, so it's lean, strong and impactful. We know you're eager to get it published, but—as we always say—it's better to get it right than rushed.

So, take a break. Set the manuscript aside for a few days or even weeks. New ideas will probably pop into your head:

Oh, I should've added this. Or, *Man! I should've deleted that.*

Write the ideas down so you can add them to your manuscript later.

Then, after your break, when your brain has rested from the intense writing, come back to your book with fresh eyes and read it all the way through. Then follow these steps:

Go back to your Summary Sentence. Does everything in your manuscript align with your Summary Sentence? If not, revise, remove, rewrite, so it's consistent from start to finish.

Remove anything extraneous. If you feel anxious about deleting words, paragraphs, or even chapters that you poured your heart into, then you can use the "strikethrough" function on your computer: ~~Sally finally quit the soul-sucking job.~~

You can also cut out the section and paste it into a file called "Book Scraps" with the date. Another idea? Save your first draft as "original," then copy it and rename it, "BOOK NAME—EDITING" with today's date. That way you can always go back to the original version if you want to retrieve something that you deleted while editing. This will alleviate anxiety during this process.

Note: You can never make too many back-up copies of your manuscript.

While writing and editing, Elizabeth saves back-up versions every few hours. Back when she was writing *Twilight* with Billy Dee Williams on a tight deadline, her computer crashed. Days' worth of intense writing disappeared! And she had to *rewrite* it all! After that, she began backing up all writing on flash drives every few hours, then at the end of each writing day. Other back-up methods include saving your manuscript on your Google Drive, your Microsoft OneDrive, and/or an external hard drive. You can also email the manuscript to yourself as an attachment. Some writers prefer to work in Google Docs, which saves all previous versions of your manuscript. Choose a method that's best for you.

Years ago, before the Internet, our dear friend's home burned down, destroying their many paper manuscripts. If your manuscripts are on paper with no digital back-up, have them transcribed into a digital format as soon as possible. You'll need that to publish them, and it's a more secure method of storage.

Let's get back to editing. Make sure you clear time and space for this important phase for your book. You need to fully immerse in reviewing your manuscript with no distractions. Turn off your devices, let folks know you're unavailable, get good sleep, eat healthy brain and body fuel, stay hydrated, and energize with exercise.

Editing, like writing, is intense, and you need to remember every detail as you proceed. When you do, watch for redundancies, repetition, extraneous information, confusing passages, and anything that feels like it's dragging. Remember while you're reading that **if you're bored, your reader will be bored.** They will put the book down. End of story.

While you're editing, ask:

- Is anything missing?

- Have current events altered my message or intention?

- Use or create an Editing & Review System that suits your style. This can include:

- Using the "show mark-up" function that changes the color of whatever you add or change, indicates the exact change in the margin, and provides space in the margin to write notes to yourself. Likewise, changes made by anyone who works on your manuscript will show up in the margin.

- Making your changes in a different color font.

- Printing the manuscript and using a pen and/or colored pens to mark it up and write changes in the white space. Then you can use them to edit the digital document.

Know that printing a physical copy of the manuscript and reviewing the black words on white paper has a way of making typos and errors jump out. Sometimes screens can be entrancing, making it easy to miss mistakes.

On the electronic version of your manuscript, you can also indicate where you want to insert photos, graphics, etc. At Two Sisters, we highlight notes to the graphic designer in yellow within the manuscript. For example:

Insert photo #12 here.

Then we share the numbered photos in Dropbox, along with a Microsoft Word document that contains numbered captions that correspond to the photos. You can also insert the photos and captions directly into the manuscript, but your graphic designer will need the high-resolution images sent separately as well.

Working with Editors

Very importantly, get a professional viewpoint. This could include a manuscript evaluation from a professional book editor. They will provide a detailed critique on your strengths and weaknesses, and how you can improve. They'll also highlight any areas that may have been crystal clear in your mind as you wrote, but read as fuzzy or confusing. When you *confuse*, you *lose* the reader's attention and your credibility crashes.

Likewise, factual errors could erode your reader's trust in you as the authority on your topic. Notice that the word "author" is inside "authority. If this happens, the reader may begin to question everything else in the book. Do your research to make sure that everything in your book is correct or hire a fact-checker.

When Elizabeth wrote *Twilight* with Billy Dee Williams, he wanted the book set in Brazil. Without a budget to travel there for a research trip—and before the Internet!—Elizabeth read books and listened to audiotapes to learn about the culture, climate, history, religion, and cuisine. After the book was published, a Brazilian person read the book and asked, "When did you visit Brazil?" That was amazing affirmation that the storytelling was authentic and accurate. So, when writing in unfamiliar territory, do your research and have an expert review it to make sure it's correct.

It's best to get a manuscript evaluation from an editor who can guide you to revise the manuscript and review the improved drafts, and see you all the way to publication or submission. Your editor can provide line editing as well as developmental editing for consistent style, structure, and content.

If you're working with a literary agent, they can provide constructive feedback on how to make your manuscript most marketable and valuable for a book deal. Then if you get a book deal at a major publishing house, you will be assigned to an editor who will guide your manuscript to publication. If you plan to submit your manuscript to a hybrid publisher or indie press, talk with them about what editing services are included in their publishing process.

If you're self-publishing, you **must** have your book pro-fessionally edited.

Unfortunately, on more than one occasion, a self-published author has gifted Elizabeth with their book. But their punctuation was such a mess that Elizabeth—an absolute stickler for commas and quote marks being used correctly—had to look away from the jumble of jacked-up symbols and messy spacing and even spelling errors. *No!* Zero chance of reading that book. And how sad, because that author had so proudly shared it, after investing the immeasurable time, effort, hope, energy, and money into writing and publishing their book. Don't let that be you! So don't do this alone!

You need a team of professionals to create and present a top-notch book to the world. It's worth every dime to invest in the best possible product that represents you and makes you proud, and makes people *want* to read your book.

A good editor can review, flag, and/or correct all grammar, punctuation, nuances, cultural sensitivities, legalities, and accuracy. They will see double meanings that you never considered, and point out passages that may seem clear to you, but confusing to your reader. Likewise, your editor should filter everything through cultural sensitivities that, if not corrected, could get you "canceled," accused of cultural appropriation, or labeled with a long list of words that could taint your image as an author.

Our editors at Two Sisters have an eagle eye for spotting outdated words that describe ethnic groups, phrasing that could feel insensitive for LGBTQ+ people, and wording that might seem condescending to a particular group. This is not the "writing police." This is insurance that you will not inadvertently alienate your readers or jeopardize your success.

Here are the types of editors you can work with:

• A **developmental editor** shapes the book.

• A **line editor** refines the language.

- A **copy editor** corrects the mechanics.

- A **proofreader** catches the last mistakes.

Now let's demystify the book-editing process.

Types of Book Editing

1. Developmental Editing

> **What is it?** Big-picture editing that looks at the *structure, content,* and *direction* of the book.

It focuses on:

- Your organization and flow.
- How you order and pace your chapters.
- Whether your story arc, theme, and messages are clear.
- Confusing passages, redundancies, holes in the narrative.
- Whether you're speaking to your target audience and optimizing your position in the marketplace.

It's best for you if: You want expert guidance on your early drafts and first manuscripts for how to shape and organize the book. Many first-time authors worry that their manuscript isn't "good enough" or that they missed something or that their writing does not sound professional or relatable. A developmental editor can help resolve that and identify how to improve the book.

2. Structural Editing

> **What is it?** Editing that focuses specifically on how the book is *built.* This is sometimes included in developmental editing.

It focuses on:

- Your sections, chapters, and subsections.
- How you use transitions between chapters.
- Your logical progression of ideas or scenes.

It's best for you if: Your manuscript has good content but feels disorganized. This is a very common concern for first-time authors, who are so immersed in their material that they "can't see the forest for the trees." Thankfully, a good editor brings expertise and new eyes and insight to the manuscript to help the author get clarity and re-structure the book if necessary.

3. Line Editing

What is it? Sentence-level editing that improves *how the writing sounds and reads.*

It focuses on:

- Your tone and voice.
- The cadence and clarity of your sentences.
- Your word choice and repetition.
- Flow from one sentence to the next sentence.

It's best for you if: Your writing is strong but you want it professionally polished to make it engaging, smooth, and compelling.

4. Copyediting

What is it? Technical editing for correctness and consistency.

It focuses on:

- Your grammar, punctuation, and spelling.

- Whether you stayed consistent in style, capitalization, and, for example, italicizing book titles.
- Checking facts.
- Whether you complied with style guidelines as provided in, for example, *The Chicago Manual of Style* or the *Modern Language Association Handbook*.

It's best for you if: Your manuscript is structurally solid and ready for accuracy checks.

5. Proofreading

What is it? The final quality check *after* the graphic designer formats the book covers and interior for printing.

It focuses on:
- Finding typos.
- Honing in on formatting errors, such as a missing indent.
- Noticing if words are missing.
- Confirming the accuracy of page numbers, scene and chapter headers, and the book's layout.

It's best for you if: Your final files are ready before the book is printed or the eBook is published.

Optional / Specialized Editing

6. Sensitivity Editing reviews content for cultural accuracy, bias, and respectful representation. This is especially important if you have people or characters in your book who have physical disabilities and/or are part of a group that has been oppressed and misunderstood.

7. Fact-Checking verifies names, dates, statistics, quotations and claims, which are common in memoirs and nonfiction.

8. Manuscript Evaluation, also known as an **Editorial Assessment**, involves a professional editor who provides a written critique of your manuscript with recommendations— but no direct editing.

A Word of Warning about Who's Invited onto Your Book-Writing Journey

Of course you want to share the thrill of writing a book with your inner circle. However, not everyone will celebrate you. If you have family members, colleagues, or even friends/ frenemies who may get jealous, resentful, or discouraging, *don't* tell them that you're writing a book. Otherwise, their negative reactions could derail you. Even if they mean well, they may be filtering your good news through their lens of biases, agendas, and what *they think* is best for you. You know who these people are, and you know *how* they are.

Writing a book can be a very vulnerable journey, and you need to maintain a confident, courageous mindset to write from your strongest, boldest voice. Unfortunately, if naysayers fill your mind with doubt, insecurity, and fear, then your writing flow could get stuck on all that mental debris and give you a bad case of writer's block that never goes away. That means you'll never write your book, and that you allowed *them* to block your dream.

What's the solution? Write your book your way and invite these people to celebrate at your book launch party.

This is not always as easy as it sounds. You may venture into a gray area if you're writing about your family, friends, faith community, and/or colleagues. If you mention them in your book, and if you reveal information that could be harmful— emotionally, professionally, or even legally—then contemplate how you will alert them that this is coming. Sometimes it's okay to allow someone to read the passages in your book that pertain to them. You are *not* asking permission. You're providing this courtesy, and you can choose to revise your manuscript if they make requests—or not. It's your book. *You* decide how to balance between the integrity of telling your truthful story versus whatever consequences may occur as a result.

And if you allow these individuals to read your manuscript before it's published, be prepared for them to potentially get angry and draw giant red X marks with all-caps demands to delete lines, paragraphs, stories and/or sections. This can be very upsetting if it involves a person close to you whose opinion matters. The bottom line, however, is that the content of your book is not *their* decision. It's *yours.*

When in doubt about how your book could impact individuals and potentially put you at risk for a defamation lawsuit, ask a lawyer. And of course, if someone threatens your personal safety if you write about them in your book, that is a grave consideration that you must resolve personally and possibly with law enforcement. Your safety comes first, so decide accordingly.

Less is More—Trim the Fat with Literary Liposuction

Elizabeth coined the term "Literary Liposuction" while editing her own books and our authors' books. Literary Liposuction means trimming the flab from a manuscript. Flab includes: using too many words that could be summarized in a word or phrase; redundancies; and sentences or paragraphs that don't move the book forward and instead cloud the message or stall the story.

Even seasoned writers compose manuscripts that require trimming. It's really fun to suction out extraneous passages, tighten the writing, and create a lean, strong, sculpted manuscript that flexes your storytelling and/or life-changing guidance.

Here's an example that we created to demonstrate Literary Liposuction.

First draft, flabby: The stars could be seen in the night sky that was very clear because no clouds from the earlier storm were blocking the view and the the whole sky looked really black and clean, which made the stars appear even brighter, like they were twinkling and glowing like there were jewels in a jewelry box. It made me feel like I could reach up and pluck a diamond out of the sky.

Revised, concise: The stars twinkled in the black velvet sky as if the clouds and rain had cleansed the skies to reveal a celestial jewelry box offering its sparkling gems for me to reach up and pluck a diamond from the heavens.

What changed?

First draft: The stars *could be seen* in the night sky that was very clear because no clouds from the earlier storm were blocking the view and *the the* whole sky looked really black and clean, which made the stars appear even brighter, like they were twinkling and glowing like *there were* jewels in a jewelry box. It made me feel like I could reach up and pluck a diamond out of the sky.
72 words

Edited, concise: The stars *twinkled* in the black velvet sky as if the clouds and rain had cleansed the skies to reveal a celestial jewelry box offering its sparkling gems for me to reach up and pluck a diamond from the heavens.
40 words

Notice the impact of replacing "could be seen" with "twinkled." First, three passive words condense into one active verb. Second, "twinkled" energizes the sentence, adds visual texture, and evokes a playful vibe. Next, look at how we replaced the repetition of "jewels in a jewelry box" with "celestial jewelry box," which removes the repetition of "jewels."

Remember that **less is more.** So identify where and how you can say the same or more with less. For example: "It made me feel like I could reach" becomes "for me to reach up."

Here's another example that we composed to demonstrate this concept:

> **First draft, telling:** When David entered the party, he *looked* around the room and *saw* a lot of well-dressed people eating and drinking and posing as if waiting for someone to take their picture for Instagram posts, but what he saw next made his heart race: the aura of a woman by the window that drew him like a moth to a flame because in his intuition he *felt* that she was his soul mate and lifelong love.
> *75 words*

> **Revised, showing:** When David entered the party, the crowd of stylish and camera-ready poseurs *blurred* in his periphery as his heart raced with *knowing* that the woman by the window—whose aura was attracting him like a moth to a flame—was his soul mate and lifelong love.
> *46 words*

Notice that removing "looked," "saw," and "felt" streamlined the sentence and shorted it by almost half its original length, which packs are more powerful punch.

Replace "ly" Words with Better Verbs

When you find yourself using an "ly" word, that's a red flag for flab. It indicates that you need to find a better verb to convey your idea with more pizzazz.

What are "ly" words? They're adverbs that emphasize the action of the verb. It's not incorrect to use adverbs. But they are clunky and indicate room for improvement. Chances are, you can say much more with fewer words when you replace these adverb phrases with strong verbs. Here are examples:

She could be seen walking slowly and seductively.
She sauntered.

He looked at her annoyedly.
He scowled at her.

Now it's your turn. Replace the passive verbs and adverbs with power verbs.
Passive: *Esmerelda could be seen running quickly.*
Active: _____

Watch for Redundancies

These are fun, and most people say these phrases every day without realizing that they are redundant. While writing, these phrases can clog your sentences.

She had a smile on her face. * She smiled.
We don't smile with any other part of the body, so smile implies the face.

He shrugged his shoulders. * He shrugged.
Similarly, we only shrug our shoulders.

There is plenty of ample parking at the store. * The store offers ample parking.
Replace the passive "there is" with a stronger verb: "offers." And since "plenty" and "ample" are redundant, select one.

Joe was eating the food. * Joe was eating.

If Joe were eating a rock or something unusual, then say that. But eating implies food. The same goes for drinking.

I thought to myself. * I thought.
We don't think to others unless we're telepathic.

She hates the taste of onions in her mouth. * She hates the taste of onions.
She wouldn't hate the taste of onions on her elbows or else-where; we only taste with our mouths, so we don't have to state it.

Beware of Bricks

It's common for first-time authors to compose first drafts that contain giant paragraphs that lack dialogue. These paragraphs appear as what we call "bricks" of words, and they are visually unappealing.

Think of a bunch of grapes. You don't put the whole bunch in your mouth at once. You enjoy one grape at a time. Likewise, you don't eat a whole loaf of bread. You pull off pieces or cut slices, then savor each bite.

Apply this idea to your book. You want your reader to take bite-sized pieces and savor the texture and flavor of each word, sentence, line of dialogue, paragraph, and idea.

You can compare this concept to a person who talks really fast and non-stop. Too much information bombards your brain and it's impossible—and undesirable—to process or retain everything they're saying. At some point, you may tune out altogether as they ramble on. Don't allow this to happen with your writing. How can you prevent it?

Use shorter paragraphs. They are more visually inviting and engaging. The white space around them frames the words so that the reader's eyes and brain can receive them more easily. To ensure this, instruct your graphic designer to typeset your book with adequate spacing between the lines and a font size that's appealing to the eyes. Most people do not want to read a single-spaced book or tiny font. If you format your book this way, you'd better have an audiobook so people can *listen* to your book rather than read it.

Shorter sentences with more white space accelerate action and heighten drama. So **vary the length and structure of your sentences**. For example:

> *I'm cold!* Sarah thought, feeling sad on a snowy February evening. *And I need a hug.* But she was alone. As tears blurred the room around her, something glimmered on her dresser—the metallic bag containing her birthday gift from a friend. *The weighted blanket!* She pulled it from the bag and heaved its twenty-five pounds of powder-blue plushness onto her bed. Then she snuggled under it. *Bliss!* She closed her eyes and sighed, loving how its velvety weight embraced her like a warm hug.

Use dialogue. It's very common when we receive manuscripts by first-time authors, that they *describe* a conversation rather than *showing* it with actual dialogue. Dialogue is far more interesting because it puts the ideas into each person's own words, plus it adds visual variety. Imagine that your friend tells you, "My boss and the CEO had an argument and really went at it with insults like you wouldn't believe." Don't you want to know exactly what they said? Details, please!

When it comes to people talking in a story, show, don't tell, by using actual dialogue rather than narration. You don't have to use dialogue for every conversation. However, it's best to use dialogue for verbal exchanges that are emotional, pivotal, unique, and relevant to your storytelling.

Very importantly, dialogue reveals the personality of the person who's speaking. Here are examples:

Narration: She told her kids to stop jumping on the couch.
Dialogue: "That couch ain't no trampoline! Yawl stop!"

Narration: Frederick had a hard time speaking the words to tell his longtime employee and friend John that he was fired.
Dialogue: "I- I- I don't . . . I'm not . . . I'm so sorry," Frederick stammered. "John, listen, I have to tell you . . . I don't, well . . . the company is—" he put his hands to his face for a moment, then stared into John's eyes. "They're . . . letting you go."

Do you see how much more interesting it is to read the vivid dialogue as opposed to a watered-down *description* of it? And do you see how the dialogue brings each character's emotions and personality to life? Clearly the mother is upset, while Frederick is extremely uncomfortable.

Each time a new person speaks, add a paragraph break, so that their dialogue starts on its own indented line. For example:

"Joe, dude, let's go to the beach!" Sam exclaimed.
"Hell no, bruh, that shark attack!" Joe responded. "Last week, remember? Plus rip tides from the storm, and—"
"Dude!" Sam said. "Live dangerously! Don't let fear stop you from having fun."
 "Bruh! Don't let being stupid stop you from being alive!"

Notice that you don't have to add attribution like "Joe said" after every quote because it's clear to the reader when each guy is talking. Plus, when you characterize each person with unique dialogue—Sam calls his friend "dude" and Joe responds with "bruh"—the reader can easily discern who's talking. Just make sure that you make it clear to the reader who is saying what. Don't make your reader have to go back to figure it out.

The dialogue should flow clearly.

Also, don't get fancy with trying to replace "said," even if it feels repetitive. The reader knows that "said" serves a function for clarity, and fancy attribution verbs such as "expounded" or "pontificated" are distracting—unless you're deliberately using a more sophisticated writing style and/or that's how you normally express yourself. You also don't want your reader to have to stop and look up the definitions of words that you use, so know your audience and write accordingly.

Make It Flow with Transitions

During the editing process, you may notice confusing or jarring jumps from one idea to another. Now is the time to fix this with transitions.

You want your storytelling to flow so smoothly that your readers do not notice the writing, because it's gently sweeping them into a world, a concept, or a learning experience where ideas are registering in their minds and hearts. That's why it's important to use transitions to move from one concept to the next. Otherwise, your writing will feel choppy and distracting as your readers struggle to adjust to a new idea. Don't make your reader have to *work* to figure out what's going on. This is especially true with flashbacks or shifts into the next anecdote or lesson. Here are several good transition words:

- At the same time,
- Meanwhile,
- As a result,
- However,
- Moments later,
- Most importantly,
- Without warning,
- Yet,

• Likewise,
• Similarly

Another way you can alert your readers that you're moving to a new idea is to insert space between paragraphs, along with three asterisks:

***

or mini graphics/symbols of something relevant to your book, such as a tiny rose, a hammer, or a crown.

Don't Suffer From Rewrite-Itis!

Editing is fun and improves your book.

But how do you know when it's time to stop?

Sometimes a deadline dictates that. You simply run out of time before your manuscript is due to your editor, publisher, or graphic designer to meet publishing deadlines.

But sometimes, especially if you fear your book is not good enough, and you have no deadlines, it's tempting to just keep editing.

We call this "rewrite-itis"—which means excessively and incessantly revising sentences, scenes, chapters, and even the whole book.

Do this, and you'll be spinning your wheels. Wasting time and energy. Maybe doing more harm than good. And the book won't get finished or published.

Rewrite-itis is especially detrimental if you stay stuck on writing the best chapter one in the history of books, but you never finish the novel, memoir, or business book.

The best advice? **Keep writing** until you finish the book. Then edit with the tips we provide here, or send the manuscript to your editor. If you realize that you're afflicted by rewrite-itis, **stop.** Get professional feedback. Hire an editor for a manuscript evaluation and developmental editing. If you have a publisher, they will assist with polishing your manuscript for publication.

We want you to enjoy this experience and feel confident that you're publishing the best book possible. You can do it!

SECTION 5

PUBLISHING

You've got options, but which is best for you? Let's demystify the publishing process, so you can find the best home for your book where it achieves long-term success.

HOW TO PUBLISH YOUR BOOK

Should you self-publish, work with a hybrid publisher, entrust your book to an indie press, go with an academic publisher, or seek representation by a literary agent who can shop your book to major publishers in the publishing mecca of New York City?

This is a deeply personal decision, and it depends on many factors.

Elizabeth has been published by major publishers, and by our hybrid publishing company, and she has self-published. After learning a lot along the way, it's exciting to share this guidance with you, so that you can choose the best publishing path for your book.

We founded Two Sisters Writing & Publishing® because we wanted to give voice to people who might otherwise never get a publishing deal, or who did not want to embark on the steep learning curve of self-publishing, or who simply wanted a high quality, personalized, and all-inclusive publishing experience.

Another motive was that while Elizabeth had been published by "Big Five" publishers for her romantic thrillers as well as her ghostwriting projects and novellas in anthologies, her valiant efforts to secure a new literary agent and land New York book deals hit a wall. This coincided with a massive disruption in the publishing industry as technology enabled everyday people to become publishers. Hence, we discovered the global publishing and distribution platform of IngramSpark.com, and the rest is history. A history of ten years and more than seventy books, in fact.

Now our publishing is truly a family affair, as we are Two Sisters and our mother writing and publishing books.

We love having control over every aspect of publishing.

So . . . which publishing option is best for you?

This section will help you make the most informed decisions for how to publish your memoir, business book, novel, self-help book, poetry collection, or any type of book you desire.

Here Are the Five Major Ways to Get Published

1. Self-Publishing
2. Hybrid Publishing
3. Academic / University Press Publishing
4. Traditional Publishing
5. Independent (Indie) Press Publishing

Which will you pursue? Consider the following points.

The fastest and least expensive is **Self-Publishing**.

The most difficult to break into is **Traditional Publishing**.

You'll enjoy easier access with **Independent, Academic, and Hybrid Publishers and the Indie Press**.

You can invest in an all-inclusive experience with **Hybrid Publishing**.

Here's a deep dive into each option.

1. Self-Publishing

How it works: You publish your book independently, hiring professionals who include an editor and a graphic designer who can design and create your cover as well as format the interior. You can also do this yourself, but make sure it looks professional. Then you open an account to publish on platforms such as Amazon KDP or IngramSpark. You own and control every aspect of your book's creation and promotion.

Pros

- As the author, you have full creative control.
- Fast publication timeline.

- Higher royalty rates per book.
- You own all rights.
- This option is excellent for entrepreneurs, speakers, coaches, and niche audiences.
- The Print-on-Demand model means you don't have to keep inventory in your garage or basement; when people order books online, they're printed and shipped from your publishing and distribution platform such as Amazon.com.

Cons

- You pay upfront costs for everything.
- You manage marketing or hire someone to promote your book.
- Self-publishing is the least prestigious way to publish your book.
- Bookstores—independent as well as chains—will probably not automatically carry your physical book unless you contact them and convince them that you can ensure sales by having an event that you market and draw in people who will buy your book.

It's best for you if: You want speed, control, and direct access to readers.

Other Self-Publishing Options

You can make a pdf of your book and sell it from your website or through email and social media. This is the cheapest, fastest, and simplest way to publish a book.

Here's another way. If you have the ability and desire to sell and distribute your physical book yourself, you can also use a printing company to produce copies of your books that you sell at speaking events, from your website, or at vendor booths. Elizabeth has done this with great success through diggypod.com and Mays Multimedia in Detroit. In addition, this can be a valuable back-up if your usual printing and distribution channels are unavailable or delayed.

2. Hybrid Publishing

How it works: A hybrid publishing company combines elements of traditional and self-publishing. You pay the company for an all-inclusive publishing experience that includes professional editing, book cover and interior design and formatting, distribution, management of book orders, and payment of royalties. One major benefit is that you retain the rights to your book, whereas traditional publishers usually own the rights to your book.

Pros

- You work with a professional publishing team.
- It's faster than traditional publishing.
- You receive higher royalties than traditional deals.
- You usually retain all rights to your book.
- You get strategic support for bestseller campaigns.
- The Print-on-Demand model means you don't have to keep inventory in your garage or basement; when people order books online, they're are printed and shipped from the publishing and distribution platform that your publisher uses, such as IngramSpark.com.
- Your book automatically appears (usually) on the major online retail sites. Each site has the discretion to carry—or not carry—your book.

Cons

- This method requires an upfront investment.
- Quality varies widely by company, so do your research!

- You'll still be involved in marketing your book.
- Bookstores—independent as well as chains—will probably not automatically carry your physical book unless you contact them and convince them that you can ensure sales by having an event that you market and draw in people who will buy your book.

It's best for you if: You prefer professional quality, guidance, speed without forfeiting full control, and a feeling that you're leaving the work to the experts.

Two Sisters publishes on the Ingram Spark Print-On-Demand platform, which means the book is part of the Ingram Book Group, the largest book distributor in the world, which has more than 39,000 outlets that include Amazon.com, Barnes & Noble's website, Apple Books, Walmart, Target, and libraries. Our authors help determine the retail sales prices of their books, which means they can purchase their hard-covers and paperbacks at wholesale cost and sell them for the cover price.

3. Academic / University Press Publishing

How it works: You submit a scholarly proposal or man-uscript to a university or academic press. These presses are operated by universities, research institutions, and academic societies. They publish books that are research-based, educational, or scholarly. Their process includes peer review and editorial board approval.

Pros

- You'll enjoy prestigious academic credibility.
- You'll receive peer-review validation.

- You can benefit from alignment with universities and institutions.
- This route is ideal for tenure, promotion, and academic authority.

Cons

- You'll face very slow timelines.
- You may receive low royalties.
- They may limit marketing to academic circles.
- You'll have minimal creative control.
- Your book may be priced too high for mainstream buyers.
- You'll still be involved in marketing your book.
- Bookstores—independent as well as chains—will probably not automatically carry your physical book unless you contact them and convince them that you can ensure sales by having an event that you market and draw in people who will buy your book.

It's best for you if: You're a professor, researcher, or scholar who's striving for academic impact, tenure, or institutional recognition—not mass sales.

4. Traditional Publishing

How it works: You submit your manuscript or book proposal to publishers (usually through a literary agent). If accepted, you sign a contract which details how the publisher will cover production costs, control most decisions, and pay an advance. An **advance** is an upfront payment that a publisher provides to an author before publication. It's paid against future royalties and recouped from the author's book sales.

Pros

- The publisher pays *you* when they purchase the rights to your book.
- You have no upfront costs.
- You usually get to work with a seasoned professional book editor and team.
- The publisher handles everything: editing, book cover and interior design, printing, distribution, and (hopefully) marketing.
- You may be assigned to a marketing associate who can orchestrate a book tour, media interviews, and other promotional events. They may also work with bookstores to place your book in high-visibility displays. Know that the publisher may only provide minimal promotions for you as an unknown, first-time author, whereas they invest heavily in marketing their top bestsellers, celebrities, and high-profile authors.
- You'll enjoy the highest prestige and credibility in the book industry.

Cons

- It's extremely competitive and nearly impossible if you don't have celebrity status, a big social following, a robust speaking platform, or extremely high-profile status in your industry.
- It may take one to three years to publish your book.
- You'll receive lower royalties
- You forfeit substantial creative control and rights.
- Unless you're a lead title, marketing support is often limited.

It's best for you if: You're seeking traditional validation, wide bookstore distribution, and/or literary prestige.

What Are the "Big Five" Publishers?

The **Big Five** are the **five largest traditional trade publishing houses in the world**. They dominate the commercial book market and control the majority of bestselling titles, bookstore distribution, major media reach, and large budgets for author advances.

When people talk about "getting a traditional publishing deal," they usually mean securing a deal with one of the Big Five. Here they are.

1. Penguin Random House
   - The largest publisher in the world.
   - They publish fiction, nonfiction, memoir, business, literary, and children's books.
   - Their authors include major celebrities, thought leaders, and prize-winning writers.

2. HarperCollins
   - They publish commercial fiction, nonfiction, memoir, faith-based, and literary titles.
   - They're known for strong distribution and brand recognition.

3. Simon & Schuster
   - They publish high-profile nonfiction, memoirs, political books, and literary fiction.
   - They often work with journalists, public figures, and established platforms.

4. Hachette Book Group
- They publish memoir, commercial fiction, lifestyle, and narrative nonfiction.
- They're known for polished production and international reach.

5. Macmillan
- They publish literary fiction, nonfiction, science, education, and popular titles.
- They're home to many award-winning and critically acclaimed books.

Each Big Five publisher owns **dozens of imprints**, which function like smaller publishing houses under one corporate umbrella.

Many authors aspire to get published by the Big Five because they can provide:

- National and international bookstore distribution.
- Access to major media outlets and reviews.
- Advance payments that are sometimes significant.
- Established and influential editorial, design, sales, and marketing teams.
- Prestige and industry credibility.

This path may perfectly align with your goals—especially if you want wide traditional exposure and are comfortable with a slower process that includes many gatekeepers.

Will the Big Five publish your book? They usually prioritize authors who already have one or more of the following:

- A **large platform** which can include prominent media presence, an established speaking audience, and a social following.
- Proven sales history.

- Celebrity or public recognition.
- Expert authority in a high-interest field.
- A concept that has broad appeal and is highly marketable.

This is why many first-time authors struggle to break in. The Big Five want to ensure a return on their investment in a new author. Having a big audience increases the chances that your book will sell well, and without that, they often do not want to take the financial risk on an unknown author.

Here's why it's very difficult to get a book deal with the Big Five:

- Most Big Five publishers **do not accept unsolicited manuscripts**, which means that if you send it to them, they will not read it. Elizabeth has seen a publisher's "slush pile" of printed manuscripts that were unsolicited (that means the publisher did not request them and they were not sent by a literary agent) and were headed for the recycling bin.
- You'll probably need a **literary agent.**
- Agents receive **thousands of submissions per year** but only select a small percentage of authors to represent.
- Big Five publishers purchase only a fraction of agented books.

Unfortunately, even if you write a brilliant book and secure a literary agent, a major publisher could reject your manuscript due to timing, market trends, and internal priorities. Despite being **highly competitive and uncertain**, authors still pursue a Big Five deal because they want:

- The potential for a lucrative book deal.
- Hopes for celebrity status, a movie deal, prestige, and credibility.
- A long-term, traditional career that grows with the

publisher's guidance.
- Placement in brick-and-mortar bookstores.
- The experience of working within the established, influential, and respected publishing system.

Literary Agents

If you're seeking a book deal with a traditional publisher, you'll need a literary agent. A literary agent is a publishing professional who represents authors and sells their books to publishers. They act as:

- Gatekeepers. They cultivate relationships with acquisitions editors who trust them to pitch only the highest quality submissions that align with the publisher's brand and imprints.
- Career advisors who can help you build long-term success.
- Contract negotiators.
- Advocates for your long-term interests.

As such, a literary agent's responsibilities include:

- Helping to refine your proposal or manuscript.
- Submitting your work to appropriate publishers.
- Negotiating advances, royalties, rights, and marketing budgets.
- Managing contracts and protecting your interests.
- Guiding your publishing career over time, such as securing multi-book contracts.
- Managing the money that you receive from your publisher, which writes a check to your agent, who then cuts a check to you after subtracting their standard 15% commission.
- Possibly working with film agents to land a movie deal for you.

You can find literary agents on the Internet as well as at in-person events such as writers conferences, literary events, and book signings. Another way is to ask other authors for referrals to their agents. You can also schedule a session with literary agents through The Detroit Writing Room and The New York Writing Room (DetroitWritingRoom.com and NewYorkWritingRoom.com).

When Elizabeth was a member of Romance Writers of America, she met agents at their annual convention where attendees signed up for author-agent appointments. She's also met agents at writers' conferences. Once, after reading an article about a prominent agent in New York, Elizabeth called their office, set up an appointment, and flew two days later to meet with them. The agent agreed to represent her project, but they left the agency before a book deal resulted.

As you seek representation with a literary agent, you can use the online submission and tracking system called **QueryTracker**, which helps you strategize, track, and organize your search. The platform enables you to:

- Search verified literary agents by genre.
- See what types of books agents are currently seeking.
- Track agents you've queried and the responses you've received.
- View response statistics and wait times.
- Read comments from other authors who are querying agents.

If you find an agent online, you'll send a short pitch email called a **query letter**. Some agents' websites request that you complete a form and upload your book proposal or manuscript. You may or may not receive confirmation that they received your submission. Or you may hear from them weeks or months later. It's common to query *dozens* of agents before a single one expresses interest.

When an agent agrees to work with you, you'll sign an **agency agreement.** Then the agent represents your work (sometimes exclusively) and submits your book to publishers. If that results in a deal, the agent negotiates terms. You want an agent who is honest and believes in your work, even when rejection letters pour in. When agreeing to work with this person, trust your gut; you will be trusting this person with your money, the fate of your book, and, if you're hoping to launch a long-term career as an author, then your professional future. That's why your agent should be strategic and should respect your creative vision.

If you want to sell your novel, you'll need to complete it, and your agent will submit it to publishers. However, if you're writing a nonfiction book, you'll need to create **a book proposal**—a professional sales document that your agent will use to pitch your book idea to publishers. Most nonfiction books are sold on proposal, not as completed manuscripts. Your proposal will show why the book should exist, who will buy it, and why you're the best person to write it. Your proposal should contain:

- **Overview**—the big idea, promise, and hook of the book.
- **Market analysis**—who the book is for and why it's needed now.
- **Comparable titles**— similar books and how yours is different or better.
- **Author platform**— your credibility, audience, and visibility.
- **Chapter outline**—a summary of each chapter.
- **Sample chapters**—usually one to three complete chapters.

Your agent will present your proposal to publishers to generate interest and hopefully negotiate a deal. If you're super lucky, your proposal could spark a bidding war, which gives your agent leverage to ask for the highest advance and best promotions package.

After a publisher buys your book, you'll write it under contract. You'll typically receive a third of your advance upon signing the contract, a third when you deliver the manuscript, and a third when the book is published. Your payments will come from your agent, who receives checks from your publisher. Your agent works on commission only, typically fifteen percent of your advance royalties, and any other deals they may negotiate, such as foreign rights and film rights. A legitimate agent never charges upfront fees such as a "reading fee" or a retainer. They get paid when you get paid.

Get the Inside Scoop

Another useful resource is **Publishers Marketplace**, a professional publishing-industry database and news platform that tracks book deals, agents, editors, and publishing trends. Authors and publishers use it to:

- See actual, current book deals (including who sold what, to which publisher, and often for how much).
- Research which agents are selling in specific genres.
- Follow editors and imprints that are actively acquiring books.
- Monitor market trends and demand by category.

Publishers Marketplace is one of the most powerful research tools if you're an author who wants to pitch strategically and secure a book deal with the Big Five.

While The Big Five represent the most traditional, prestigious, and competitive publishing route, they are not the right—or realistic—choice for every author, especially first-time writers who lack a major platform. If this sounds daunting to you, please remember that you can achieve great success, impact, and bestseller status via other publishing routes.

5. Independent (Indie) Press Publishing

How it works: An **indie press**—short for **independent press**—is a small, privately owned publishing company that provides a boutique experience with personalized attention and customized creative development. They specialize in mission-driven books and typically publish memoirs, niche nonfiction, poetry, and diverse authors with culturally relevant messages.

Pros

- You'll enjoy a more close-knit relationship with the editorial team.
- Your book will get published faster than with a traditional publisher.
- You'll also enjoy more creative freedom.
- You'll receive higher royalties than traditional publishing.
- You'll get more personalized marketing support.
- Indie presses embrace first-time authors and diverse voices.

Cons

- As a smaller company, indie presses usually have more limited marketing budgets than traditional publishers.
- They pay lower advances—sometimes no advance at all.
- They also have less influence to get your book into bookstore chains.
- Their distribution networks may be scaled down.
- Authors collaborate on promotions.

It's best for you if: You have a purpose-driven book and prefer a boutique experience with personal attention and creative development that's customized for your needs.

What about the Vanity Press?

Vanity press companies—also known as "author-services publishing" and "assisted self-publishing"—follow a business model where you as the author pay the company to publish your book and provide bundled services that can include:

- Editing that is often basic.
- Cover design that is usually from a template.
- Interior formatting.
- ISBN assignment.
- Distribution setup.
- Optional marketing packages that are usually expensive.

How do they work?

- You sign a service contract.
- You select and pay for a package.
- The company uploads the book to retailers such as Amazon or IngramSpark.
- You retain some rights, but often with **limitations or fees** to make changes later.

These companies include AuthorHouse, Xlibris, iUniverse, Balboa Press, WestBow Press, and Archway Publishing. Vanity press companies are a good option if: your book is primarily personal or legacy-driven; budget is not a concern; you prefer a hands-off experience; and you're not hoping for bestseller status.

Should You Create an Audiobook? Yes!

Many people tell us and our authors, "I don't read books. Do you have an audiobook?"

We hear this question frequently because growing numbers of people prefer to listen to the recorded version of a book while they're commuting, walking, doing chores, exercising, or relaxing. People love the ease and convenience of audiobooks because you can listen to them through apps on your phone, through downloads, and on library platforms.

As an author, it's smart to offer an audiobook version of your book because it can:

- **Expand your audience** by reaching people who prefer listening over reading.
- **Boost sales** because audiobooks add a revenue stream alongside your print and eBooks.
- **Promote discoverability** as platforms like Audible, Spotify, and Apple Books can introduce your work to new listeners.

You'll want to take advantage of the booming audiobook market, with U.S. sales increasing by 50% from 2020 to 2025, according to Libro.FM blog.[1] Projections show that audiobook revenue will surge to $11 billion in 2026, and $35 billion in 2030, when audiobook sales are expected to represent 21% of global publishing revenue, up 12% from 2021.[2]

Clearly, it's very beneficial for you to create an audiobook version of your memoir, business book, self-help book, novel, poetry collection, or other type of book.

But how do you create an audiobook? If you have a publisher, they can advise you and potentially oversee this process. Many of our authors hire voice actors from the production platform called ACX.com (Audiobook Creation Exchange), which distributes your book to Audible, Amazon, and iTunes. This way, your audiobook will show up beside the hardcover, paperback, and eBook versions of your book on Amazon.

What if you want to record your book in your own voice? You can, but it's not as easy as it sounds. You'll need to rent a studio, hire a sound engineer and editor, and spend *many* hours recording as you read your book. And you don't just *read* your book. You need to sound energetic—not monotone—with intonations that are appropriate for each scene. You also need to read in a way that distinguishes different voices of people in your book. Not to mention, our mouths make a lot of sounds that we're not aware of—and those sounds can be very unpleasant for the listener.

That's why our advice is to leave it to the experts. You can hire a narrator on ACX in two ways: pay their hourly rate so you can keep all royalties, or pay nothing up front and pay them 50% of royalties. On ACX.com, you can search through an impressive selection of voice actors by filtering exactly what you're seeking, such as: female, African American, conversational, high energy.

A Word of Warning

PLEASE do your research regarding any person or company you work with during your quest to write, publish, and promote your book! This includes editors, agents, publishers, independent contractors, book coaches, graphic designers, publicists, social media managers, and any person whom you might pay to provide services for your book.

It's best to get word-of-mouth recommendations from people you trust *before* you sign a contract and pay someone. You should also get everything in writing because clear written agreements protect expectations, timelines, deliverables, and finances; they prevent misunderstandings and safeguard your rights and investment. You can use an online service such as RocketLawyer.com to craft a simple legal agreement that you and the other person can sign electronically. Do not make verbal agreements, even with friends, and do not pay anyone before you sign a contract.

We've heard too many horror stories from authors who paid large sums of money to independent contractors and companies that failed to deliver or engaged in unscrupulous practices that left the author frustrated, financially depleted, and even bookless. Even worse, some discover that the rights to their own book are entangled in a contract, leaving them legally unable to publish it themselves or with another company.

How Will You Publish Your Book?

You're in the driver's seat to navigate the best route to reach your destination as a published author.

- If you want **impact + income**, then self-publishing or hybrid publishing are best for you.
- If you're aiming for **tenure + scholarly credibility**, then the academic press your ideal solution.
- If you're seeking **prestige + bookstores**, then opt for a traditional publisher.

Now that you understand the many paths available to publish your book, know this: **you can do it!** You have the power to choose the route that best aligns with your goals, your values, and your vision—and to define success on your own terms. Whether your dream is to change lives, build a business, leave a legacy, or simply hold your story in your hands, your success is created by the clarity of your choices and your courageous quest to turn your book dreams into published reality.

SECTION 6

PROMOTING & PROFITING

The time is now to start building your tribe and alerting your readers about the release of your book. This will have a ripple effect that builds awareness about your book for readers everywhere. Your promotions can help generate profits, enabling you to earn a return on your investment (ROI) with public speaking, bulk sales, and online courses.

PROMOTE, PROMOTE, PROMOTE!

Alert & Activate Your Networks to Promote Your Book & Maximize Sales

It's never too soon to start promoting your book. In this section, you'll learn how to create and launch a promotions strategy that increases your chances of becoming a bestseller, and we'll explain what that entails. We'll also help you plan your book launch and sustain attention that generates book sales and a return on your investment.

Your Pre-Publication Promotion Strategy

If you have a book deal with a major publisher, please work with their marketing team to collaborate on the best promotions strategy for your book. Unless you're super famous and they're investing a big budget into your promotions plan—with a multi-city tour, top television morning show guest appearances, and high-profile book signings—you will still need to market your book through your personal and professional networks, as well as via social media and in-person events.

Similarly, if you're going to publish with a hybrid publisher or indie press, please also collaborate with them to supplement their promotions plan. Knowing your Intention for your book is crucial so that you can customize your book launch and subsequent publicity accordingly.

If you plan to self-publish, and you're not going to hire a publicist, then you are your own marketing director.

When you wrote your Summary Sentence, you defined your motivation for writing and publishing a book. This is deeply personal and dramatically varies for every author. So, stick to yours and believe in it with every ounce of your being.

Many authors feel that the act of publishing a book is an accomplishment unto itself; they are not seeking public fanfare or accolades or bestseller status. Others don't even publish for the public and quietly share their books with family members only.

However, many authors *do* want to become bestsellers for the status, marketplace affirmation, and profits that result. The following information caters to those individuals, so feel free to use any ideas that align with your Summary Sentence.

At the same time, some authors do not want to participate in the big-business monopoly of book sales by bookstore chains and mammoth online retailers. They prefer to support small business booksellers and/or sell the book themselves from a website or at their speaking events. If that's your preference, go for it!

When you defined your Intention, you may have written "become a bestselling author" and even rank on *The New York Times* Best Sellers list. Here's guidance on how to achieve that.

Note: *If striving for best seller status does not interest you, please skip the following sections and proceed to "2. Book Branding & Metadata."*

Why Seek Bestseller Status?

Becoming a *New York Times* bestselling author is extremely prestigious and indicates that your book has achieved extraordinary visibility and distribution. It also means that you have struck a powerful chord with readers, and sales are booming. Why? Because your NYT bestseller ranking means your book sold enough copies within a specific category to rank against other titles during the week that the list was compiled.

A NYT bestseller designation can dramatically elevate you by attracting national media attention, lucrative speaking engagements, opportunities to lead corporate consulting, invitations to speak at universities, and more sales involving bookstores, libraries, and bulk buyers. For many authors, these perks define the pinnacle of success with traditional publishing.

Unfortunately, it's very difficult to rank on The New York Times Best Sellers list, even if you sell a lot of books. *The Times* list is curated with a confidential methodology that combines sales data from a limited group of retailers, along with human analysis by *New York Times* editors. In addition, this exclusive list often favors large publishers and specific retailers. This makes the list unattainable for most authors.

That said, it *is* possible for you to become an Amazon best-selling author. When your book reaches bestseller status on Amazon, it indicates that readers are responding, your marketing is working, and your launch was successful. This ranking creates instant social proof, elevates your book in the Amazon algorithm, and gives you credibility-boosting bragging rights that you can use in media pitches, speaker bios, book covers, and promotions.

An Amazon bestseller can really amplify your influence, prosperity, and credibility especially if you're an entrepreneur, coach, speaker, or thought leader.

Becoming an Amazon Bestseller

How can you become a bestselling author on Amazon? Here is a promotions strategy that has launched many of our Two Sisters authors onto the Amazon bestsellers lists in multiple categories for each format of their book in hardcover, paperback, and eBook. You can follow this plan to increase your chances of achieving bestseller status.

1. Timeline & Strategy

- Start three to six months before your publication date.

- Choose a specific launch week. You'll have the best success by publishing your book on a Tuesday, Wednesday or Thursday.

- Decide whether you are targeting:

- A specific Amazon bestseller category (such as memoir or spiritual self-help).

- #1 New Release status.

- Overall Amazon rank. This is more difficult, but it's possible when you generate strong traffic.

2. Book Branding & Metadata

Brainstorm Your Branding

Whether you want to go global with your book or privately share it with your inner circle, your book's appearance, style, and feel should align with and showcase your personal and professional branding.

For example, the cover design of award-winning *Joy Notes: Balancing the Trauma with Triumph* by Niobis Queiro is purple because that's her favorite color and it's her brand color as a motivational speaker. The cover of her Cuban-Spanish translation has the same design.

We are so proud that the Cuban-Spanish version of Nio's book—*Notas de Alegria: Equilibrar el trauma con el triunfo*—was released in October 2025 as Two Sisters' first Spanish-language translation. This bolsters Nio's brand and expands her influence as an author, because she wanted to honor her Cuban American family heritage as well as appeal to her large following of Spanish-speaking readers.

Likewise, Elizabeth's personal style of dress, as well as her professional branding for her Goddess Power podcast, YouTube channel, social media posts, and website all feature sparkly animal prints and a smoky purple background. So, it was only natural that her Goddess Power book covers showcase this aesthetic.

If you're starting a new brand with your book, conduct market research by studying popular cover designs and styles to understand why and how they appeal to readers. But just because something is popular, doesn't mean you should use it, especially if you don't even like it. Go with what appeals to *you*.

You can also study the psychology of colors as it pertains to branding, and specifically to book cover design. For example, a business or leadership book often uses **blue** on the cover to convey trust, clarity, and credibility, helping readers feel confident in the guidance inside. A motivational or high-energy business book may use **red** to incite urgency and bold action, alerting readers that the content is curated to motivate movement and results. Make sure you choose colors that *you* like.

Likewise, select fonts that are appropriate for your book. Do you want a formal script? Or big, playful letters? What about a standard font that will lend credibility to your business book?

Apply this thinking to your title on the cover as well as to the font that you select for the chapter headings and text inside your book. Be aware that some fonts are pretty and fun, but difficult to read. If your potential readers have to struggle to decipher your title, they won't. They'll put the book down. Therefore, err on the side of simplicity and clarity rather than cuteness or experimental styles.

Do you have a business logo? Align your book cover design and all promotional materials with the color and style of your logo. This will enable you to cross-pollinate all your endeavors by creating recognizable images that create consistency and an endless loop that boosts your brand.

Likewise, your author photo should reflect the tone, style, and content of your book. Is it professional, authoritative, sultry, playful, rebellious, romantic? Sassy, serious, somber, sarcastic?

At the same time, stay consistent with your artwork, photos, and images on all promotional materials. For example, your photos, videos, and images could all be: black and white; colorful to reflect your brand; cheerful, such as smiling people; and/or symbolic of your message. For example, your book is about make-up, then lipstick, eyelashes, bronzers, and eyeliners can dominate the imagery.

Work with a professional graphic designer to create your **book cover**. This is imperative because people *do* judge a book by its cover. Investing in the cost of graphic design, which includes the interior formatting of your book, will pay off because you want your book to look as professional as possible.

When Catherine published her 2017 Young Adult series, *The Veronica Series*, she hired a graphic design firm called 1106 Design to create book covers that are fun, colorful, and appealing to young teenaged girls.

The cover of Book 1, *Veronica, I Heard Your Mom's Black*, features shades of purple and blue with a whimsical font and the silhouette of a girl's profile with flowers in her hair. Book 2, *Veronica Talks to Boys*, is green and blue with a similar profile that includes a boy's face. And Book 3, *Race Home, Veronica*, shows the side view of a girl riding a bike with a green and pink design. The aesthetic is feminine and fun, and each book matches as a series.

What image or images should appear on your book cover? Study the marketplace to study similar books in your genre. Do an online search for upcoming trends in book cover design. But always follow your heart and work with your graphic designer to create a book cover that reflects you and your brand. Your cover image can be a photo of you, or something symbolic of your message. For example, *Joyously Free* is a burst a rainbow-colored clouds; it's eye-catching, conveys the joy of the book's mission, and symbolizes LGBTQ+ Pride.

Your book cover will also require an alluring **synopsis** that convinces your target audience that they *need* your book as the ultimate solution to a problem that's been vexing them. Multi-purpose this synopsis by using it:

- As the back cover text on your book; and

- As the book's description on your website, on Amazon, on social media, in email blasts, and in press releases. Later you'll read about the importance of using keywords that inspire the online algorithm to direct your content to people who are seeking it.

If you're aiming for Amazon bestseller status, write a compelling Amazon book description using keywords. Here's where AI such as ChatGPT can help, because it will compose a keyword-rich description that inspires the algorithm to push your book toward people who are searching for content like yours.

Understanding Metadata

When we started Two Sisters Writing & Publishing®, Catherine handled the metadata when setting up our book titles on IngramSpark. Then she taught this concept to Elizabeth, who short-circuited at the very word "metadata." For someone who loves contemplating action verbs and writing sentences for hours in silence, solitude, and unbridled creativity, Elizabeth found the concept of metadata extremely technical, tedious, and confusing. However, thanks to Catherine's excellent tutorial, Elizabeth mastered this crucial step in book publishing.

The point for you is that, if anything in this writing and publishing process seems overwhelming and confusing, please stick with it, get help, and have faith that you *can* do it.

What is Book Metadata?

It's the collection of information that describes, identifies, categorizes, and markets a book, including the title, subtitle, author name, author bio, affiliations, short and long book descriptions, keywords, categories, themes, book format (hardcover, paperback, eBook, audiobook), ISBN, pricing, on-sale date, and publication date. It alerts bookstores, online retailers, libraries, and search engines what the book is, who it's for, and how to find it; this directly influences discoverability, sales, and distribution.

Your publisher will manage your metadata. However, if you're self-publishing, you'll need to collect your metadata and enter it on your publishing platform. Before you do this, you'll need to purchase and assign one ISBN for each format of your book—paperback, hardcover, eBook, and audiobook.

The ISBN appears in the bar code on the back of the book. It is your International Standard Book Number; just like Americans have a social security number as their government-issued identification, every book has a **unique 13-digit identifier**. ISBNs are used by publishers, bookstores, libraries, and distributors to identify, track, order, and sell that book accurately. Your publisher will assign ISBNs to each format of your book. If you're self-publishing, the official place to purchase ISBNs is Bowker.com. You can buy one or you can save significant money by purchasing them in blocks of ten, 100, or 1,000.

Your metadata includes categories and keywords, which help online sites organize where to place your book, and which bestseller lists are relevant for your content. If you have a traditional, academic, or indie publisher, they will determine this for you.

At Two Sisters, we love working with our authors to curate the best selection of categories. Teamwork makes the dream work, so make sure you're working with a company or individual(s) who welcome your input if you want to give it. Some authors don't want to be involved and leave the details to us as the experts.

You'll need to create your Amazon Author Page in Author Central. This is your showplace for your books, bio, pictures, videos, and messages to readers; you can introduce yourself and your books to them and cultivate relationships with fans to lay a strong foundation for your publishing career with credibility and interactive communication. You must create your Amazon Author Page yourself; your publisher cannot do it for you.

We also highly recommend that you open author accounts on **Goodreads.com** and **BookBub.com.**

Our book give-away contests on Goodreads have engaged thousands of readers who want to win each author's book! These contests and the book on Goodreads boost visibility and excite people to buy it. Goodreads is "the" place for you as an author, because it has more than 150 million registered members around the world. As one of the biggest book-focused online communities, Goodreads enables you to connect with readers, garner reviews, and build awareness for your book(s).

Likewise, BookBub is a book-promotion and discovery platform that helps readers find deals and recommendations. As an author, you can promote your book with targeted ads and featured promotions to attract highly engaged readers.

3. Website & Pre-Orders

A major publisher, indie press, and hybrid publisher will feature and sell your book on their website. However, if you're self-publishing, you'll need to create a website and process pre-orders yourself to optimize your chances of becoming an Amazon bestseller.

When you create a website, it can be as simple as a landing page that tells the world about your book, why you wrote it, why they need to read it, and how to purchase it. Include links to online sales platforms and/or an e-commerce function so you can take pre-sales and fulfill orders. If you choose to sell books without a website, you can take orders via email and process payments through cash apps, Venmo, PayPal, Zelle, or other digital payment platforms.

Your website will need:

- Your book description.

- Your author bio. This may be different than a professional bio that you may use for your career. For example, if you're a real estate agent by day and romance author by night, then you'll want to create a bio that highlights why you write romance. However, if your real estate life intersects with your storytelling—perhaps your heroine is a luxury home broker who falls in love with the forbidden fruit of her top competitor or biggest client—then wrap it all together in an upbeat bio. Your readers want to know about you as the author, so flex your creativity in your bio. You'll be repurposing your author bio many times—in your book, on your Amazon author page, in the metadata if you use IngramSpark, and on promotional materials—so make it sparkle!

- An email signup function. You can have a "pop up" feature on your website that captures email addresses with a simple invitation to join your email list, receive a newsletter, or download a free pdf or coupon that's relevant to the book.

- Pre-order links. This should be bold and placed at the top of your page with a direct link to pre-order your book on Amazon.

Your book must be uploaded well before your publication date to allow time for pre-orders to build. This is imperative for your bestseller strategy.

Use your website as your single hub for all promotion. Drive traffic there by putting the link on your social media pages and in the signature block of your emails. You can also blog regularly with SEO-rich content that can help elevate your website's ranking on search engines.

4. Alert & Activate Your Networks to Build Your Audience

The first people who purchase your book will probably be your family members, friends, colleagues, and professional communities who want to support and celebrate your publishing dream. That's why it's important to start your promotions with people who already know, like, and respect you. Your promotions plan starts here. Now's the time to identify these individuals and groups, and let them know that you're writing a book.

Our bestselling author Joanie Lindenmeyer made pink business cards that say, "I'm writing a book!" She handed them out to people she met in restaurants, the grocery store, church, events, airports, you name it. She also emailed family members and friends across America to announce that she was writing a memoir called *Nun Better: An Amazing Love Story* that would be published on March 19, 2023, a day that is special to her story.

Now it's time to identify your personal and professional associations and affiliations. If you'd like to recruit your friends and fans to volunteer for your book launch/promotions team, reach out to people who may want to do this. These ambassadors will readily support your request to help plan and host your book launch event(s). They may also help you promote the book and spread the word via newsletters, email blasts, social media postings, events, and of course, pre-orders for your book.

Name key supporters in your personal network of friends & family:

_____

_____

_____

Neighborhood associations:

_____

_____

_____

Faith communities:

_____

_____

_____

Alumni associations:

_____

_____

_____

Sorority/Fraternity:

_____

_____

_____

Support groups:

_____

_____

_____

Groups for sports, hobbies, recreation:

_____

_____

_____

Professional Organizations

_____

_____

_____

Craft Your Messaging

Now let's list the groups of people in your professional and community networks who could potentially support and help promote your book.

Write a template email announcement about your book that includes:

- The title.
- A brief description of the book that emphasizes what's in it for them.
- The publication date.
- Your book cover, when you have it.

- The link to pre-order, if you have it. Or tell them when you can share it.
- The CTA, Call to Action, requesting their support to pre-order the book, forward this email, share this announcement in their newsletter, post it on their website and social media or whatever forum is appropriate, invite you to speak and have a book signing, host an event for you such as a "Chat with the Author" or speaking engagement at your alma mater. The list is endless.

Be creative and bold!

Don't be afraid to ask for help. And remember that your book won't sell itself. You need people to buy it, read it, and spread the word! People in your networks already know and like you, so they'll be eager to help. But you have to *ask* first.

We're providing this template email announcement that you can revise to fit your communication style. You can also create several versions for specific groups, such as: family members, business colleagues, close friends, acquaintances, and others.

Email Subject Line: Exciting news! My book is coming soon

Dear [Name],

I hope this note finds you well. I'm reaching out because you've been part of my life in a meaningful way, and I want you to hear this exciting news directly from me.

I've been working hard to bring one of my biggest dreams to life: I wrote a book! [BOOK TITLE], will be published on [PUBLICATION DATE]. This project has been so close to my heart, and I'm thrilled to finally share it with you and the world.

The book explores [one brief sentence about what the book is about / who it's for / why it matters], and it represents important chapters of my life and work.

If you feel inspired to support me, please pre-order the book. Pre-orders build my book's early momentum and visibility, especially during launch week.

Here's the pre-order link: [INSERT LINK HERE]

I'm also starting to plan ways to celebrate and share the book, and I'd love to explore possibilities with you. If it feels aligned, I'd be honored to:

- Speak at your organization, business, alumni group, book club, or online community;
- Host a book signing or intimate book reception at your home, workplace, organization, or club;
- Offer a talk, workshop, or conversation followed by a book signing;
- Join you for an event where storytelling, inspiration, or dialogue would be welcome.

There's no pressure! This is simply an open invitation and expression of gratitude for being in my world.

Thank you for the encouragement, conversations, and connection you've shared with me over the years. It means more than I can say. I'm so grateful to experience this life with people I respect and care about.

With appreciation and excitement,
[Your Name]
[Author of BOOK TITLE]
[Website or social media link, optional]

Build an Email List to Promote Your Book

This is a powerful way to sell your book. How?

- Send regular emails featuring:

    - Save-the-date announcements for upcoming events.
    - Behind-the-scenes updates.
    - Intrigue-sparking excerpts.
    - Launch countdown reminders.
    - Special offers such as "win coffee with the author."

- Blog weekly (or bi-weekly) and email a link to your network using:

    - Book excerpts.
    - Personal stories.
    - Reflections on current events relating to your book.

Using email and blogging to promote your book during the time leading up to your publication date really works! Our author Mort Meisner blogged every week for three months prior to the 2020 release of *Enough to be Dangerous: One Agent's Life in TV News and Rock & Roll*. Each email included an excerpt from the book. He blasted it out to his contacts across America. And this launched his hardcover, paperback, and eBook to multiple bestsellers lists on Amazon as well as the rank of #1 New Release in his categories.

In every email, provide a link where people can pre-order the book. Ask them to forward the email to others who can order the book and spread the word. Some people will want to read the book because the content appeals to them, while others may simply want to support your endeavor as a published author.

5. Social Media & Visibility

Create and brand your social media platforms. You can open business pages specifically designed to market and sell your book. Then promote your new business pages on your personal accounts to drive traffic, and curate the best hashtags to reach your target audience.

Link all platforms directly to your Amazon pre-order page and/or your website. Then post consistently:

- Quotes from the book.
- Writing journey moments.
- Short videos—Instagram reels, YouTube shorts, TikTok videos. If you have a business book, post videos on LinkedIn.
- Be yourself! Even if you're new at this, people love authenticity. So express your dreams, fears, requests, revelations. Relax and have fun, always remembering *Why* you're sharing your book with people everywhere.

Start posting **at least ninety days before your publication date.**

Consider a Podcast, YouTube Channel, and Online Community

These are optional but powerful. If you create a podcast on YouTube, Spotify, Apple Podcasts, and other platforms, you can dive deep into the specific content of your book. Decide whether you want to host your episodes solo, or invite guests who provide insight into your topic, or both.

Use content to:

- Explore the themes in your book.
- Introduce yourself to future readers and invite them to join your journey by commenting and sharing their own stories and tips.
- Build trust with potential readers before you ask them to buy your book and spread the word.

6. Events & Launch Activation

Your book launch party and events that follow can be some of the most exciting experiences of becoming a published author. But first, what exactly is a book launch?

It's a strategic campaign that precedes and follows your publication date, with concentrated marketing, promotions and activities that aim to build a book-buying buzz. During this time, your mission is to gain visibility, increase your credibility, inspire reviews, and create momentum for sales. You'll want to gain traction with your book on retail sites (especially Amazon), garner opportunities for media interviews and public speaking, and establish your authority as the author of a "must read" book.

During your launch, you officially present your book to the world. This can be an intimate reception with family and friends or a public party or even a virtual event and book tour. If your book showcases your professional expertise and your target audience includes people in your industry, you could launch it at the top conference in your field. If you're a coach, time your book launch with the start of new workshops or online trainings.

You'll be in awe of the joy and celebration that your family, friends, colleagues, and fans shower on you during the official release of your book.

The book party for our author Lin Day in 2018 was so joyous! Her friends hosted a reception in their beautiful home with a lavish spread of food, cocktails and conversation on the spacious deck, then a presentation in the family room where Lin, Elizabeth, and others spoke about Lin's life and book. Lin also autographed copies of *Remembering and Forgetting: a spiritual journey*, which shares how hypnotherapy helped her remember and heal from traumas in her earlier life.

For Elizabeth, her book parties remain some of the most wonderful memories of her life. For her first bestselling novel, nearly 300 people gathered in a pretty venue where they enjoyed hors d'oeuvres and an open bar while she autographed copies for each person. For her second bestselling novel, *Dark Secret*, the party was even better, because it was on her birthday, and she autographed nearly 400 books. And for her third best-selling romantic thriller, *Twilight*, co-authored with movie star Billie Dee Williams, together they autographed 600 books in a ballroom party featuring live music, a seafood buffet with ice sculptures, limousine service, and joy that people *still* talk about to this day.

Most recently, Elizabeth launched the first book in her six-part women's empowerment series *The Biss Tribe: Where You Activate Your Goddess Power*, at a plush "Pink Party" in a cool downtown loft hosted by Detroit by Design. At this party, she also interviewed people on her podcast, The Goddess Power Show with Elizabeth Ann Atkins®.

Our mother's book launch was in the beautiful home of a dear family friend who loves to entertain on her spacious patio around her swimming pool and in her luxe party room. She provided live music, catering, a wine selection, and warm hospitality, culminating in a book signing where our mother and others shared celebratory and heartfelt comments.

Similarly, Joanie Lindenmeyer launched *Nun Better: An Amazing Love Story* at her favorite pizzeria where friends and family packed the party room that was decorated with fresh roses and balloons. A second party followed inside the plush Paschal Winery & Vineyard amidst the mountains of Southern Oregon.

Then we launched the books that Elizabeth and Joanie co-authored— *Joyously Free: Stories & Tips for LGBTQ+ People, Parents and Allies* at Motor City Pride in June of 2024 and *Healing Religious Hurts: Stories & Tips to Find Love and Peace*— at a festive party at Paschal Winery & Vineyard. Also at that gathering, Elizabeth released Book 2 in her Goddess Power book series: *The Biss Tribe: Where You Activate Your Goddess Pleasure*. We actually had *five books* at this event!

So, what do you actually *do* at a book launch? You greet your guests and thank them for supporting you. You autograph books for them, after a trusted person handles the sales for you. You and others may speak about your story, the book, and why it's important.

Dr. Robert Treuherz, author of *Ten 2nd Chances: This Doctor Died and Went to Hell, Why?* hosted a gala book launch at the UCLA Retreat Center in Lake Arrowhead, California, in October 2025. Some members of the medical team who saved his life and performed his heart transplant attended the event and spoke along with his family members who co-authored the book: wife Claudia Treuherz, son Bradley Treuherz, and son-in-law Alan Davenport. More than 100 people attended the party that featured a DJ, gourmet hors d'oeuvres, wine, and champagne in a picturesque setting.

When planning your book launch, be creative and orchestrate events that excite you! If you wrote a beauty book, host a spa day; in addition to an "author talk" about your book and your book signing, make the ticket price include a beauty treatment or massage. If your book is about sailing, host your book launch on a boat or at a marina or at a yacht club.

As with everything about your book, it's *your* creation and you have the power to launch it into the world however you desire. So, get creative and plan something that excites you and the people you're writing for.

7. Launch-Week Bestseller Push

- Coordinate:

    - Email blasts, including several during launch week.
    - Social media posts every day of launch week.
    - Personal outreach with text messages, DMs, and phone calls.

- Ask supporters to:

  - Buy your book during a 24- to 72-hour window around your publication date.
  - Write Amazon reviews after they buy the book.
  - Spread the word on their networks.
  - Host events to promote your book.
  - Post pictures of themselves with your book on their social media and make videos about why they love the book.

8. Maintaining Post-Launch Momentum

- Post photos and videos of your launch events on social media.
- Post daily social media updates about reader reactions, events, and your publishing journey.
- Continue asking for reviews.
- Share screenshots of your book on the best seller lists.
- Pitch media, podcasts, and speaking engagements that emphasize that your book is an "Amazon Bestseller."

SECTION 7

THE BUSINESS OF WRITING

Writing and publishing your book is a business decision, and understanding its financial aspects will empower you to move forward with clarity and confidence. This section gently walks you through budgeting, pricing, and planning so your book can support your dreams, your message, and your future.

THE BUSINESS AND BUDGETING FOR WRITING & PUBLISHING

Understanding The Business— and Expenses!—of Writing

Right now, your mind is probably consumed with how to actually *write* your book. However, it's important to understand the business of writing so that you can embark on this venture to optimize the financial aspects of becoming a published author. You may have a lot of questions.

Do you need an LLC?

Should you open a business bank account for expenses and profits?

How do you account for money spent and received on your annual income taxes?

What payment system will you use to process book orders on your website? What cash app will you use on your phone or computer to process sales at events? How will you track spending and profits? Who will handle your royalties? Where will they be deposited?

The answers all depend on you and your Intention for your book. We highly recommend that you consult with your trusted CPA, tax professional, or financial advisor. They know you and your financial profile, and can best assess how to proceed.

Our company actually started when we realized that we could merge Elizabeth's writing and publishing experiences with the business expertise that Catherine had gleaned during her career in the financial services industry. Plus, with Catherine also being a published author, we saw Two

Sisters Writing & Publishing® as an opportunity to publish our own books and showcase diverse authors who have fascinating, inspiring stories to share. Becoming entrepreneurs taught us what's required to launch and sustain a business, and we love to share that knowledge with our authors when they ask for guidance about the business of writing books.

Some of our authors do create an LLC with a federal tax ID number, as well as a separate business bank account with debit and credit cards. Their royalties are deposited into that account. This way, all spending and profiting related to the book are neatly contained and accounted for.

While we're on the topic of money, now is the time to understand the potential costs related to your writing and publishing venture. Determine how you want to proceed and, if necessary, start saving and/or budgeting for those expenses now. Please don't get sticker shock! You don't need *everything* on our checklist, and the expenses do not all occur at once.

Budgeting for Writing, Publishing, and Promoting Your Book

It's best to plan ahead to prepare for the financial investment of becoming a published author. Below are the main categories to consider as you create your book budget.

Writing Costs

These are the investments that support you in *creating* your book.

- Book coach.
- Ghostwriter.
- Editor.
- Getting referrals from trusted sources.
- Financing options such as investors, sponsors, or GoFundMe campaigns.

- Paying assistants who help with research, transcription, or organization.

Publishing Costs

These are the services that turn your manuscript into a professionally published book.

- Publisher or publishing services.
- ISBNs.
- Copyright registration.
- Barcodes.
- Trademarks (when applicable).
- Cover design.
- Interior formatting and layout (including photos and manuscript formatting).
- Purchasing author copies of your book.

Promoting Costs

These investments help your book reach readers.

- Publicist or PR firm.
- Social media manager.
- Website creation and maintenance.
- Marketing materials such as business cards, flyers, postcards, banners, etcetera.
- Book trailer.
- Podcasting equipment.
- Venue rentals.
- Travel to conferences, book fairs, and events.
- Marketing assistants and support staff.

Book Writing & Publishing Expenses Checklist

Here's a helpful checklist of potential expenses, presented in the order that you may need them. Please note that these are early 2026 prices.

1. The **Writing & Development Phase.** *Creating your manuscript.*

- Writing coach and/or developmental editor
  $1,500–$10,000+
- Writing conferences, workshops, retreats (travel + registration)
  $300–$3,000+
- Research expenses (books, interviews, permissions)
  $100–$1,000+
- Writing tools and software
  $0–$500

2. **Editing & Manuscript Completion.** *Polishing your book.*

- Line editor / copyeditor
  $1,000–$6,000
- Proofreader
  $500–$2,000
- Beta readers or sensitivity readers (optional)
  $0–$1,500

3. **Publishing & Production Setup.** *Turning your manuscript into a book.*

- ISBNs (author-owned, if applicable)
  $125–$575+
- Publishing and distribution setup fees
  $0–$2,000+
- Interior book design and formatting (print + eBook)
  $500–$3,000
- Professional cover design with a graphic designer
  $500–$5,000

4. Author Platform & Brand Foundation. *Establishing your public presence.*
- Author website (design, domain, hosting)
  $300–$5,000+
- Professional author photos
  $300–$1,500
- Videographer and/or book trailer
  $500–$3,000+
- Branding (logo, fonts, visual identity)
  $0–$2,500

5. Pre-Launch Marketing & Promotion. *Building awareness before release.*

- Social media or online marketing manager
  $500–$5,000/month
- Email marketing tools and list-building
  $0–$300/month
- Advance review copies (print or digital)
  $100–$1,000
- Advertising and promotions
  $300–$5,000+
- Promotional materials (cards, postcards, posters, signage)
  $100–$1,000

6. Launch & Release Events. *Celebrating and selling your book.*

- Author copies of the book
  $200–$2,000+
- Book launch party or release events
  $300–$5,000+
- Event travel and accommodations
  $300–$3,000

7. Post-Launch & Long-Term Promotion. *Sustaining awareness and sales.*

- Publicist or PR firm
  $2,000–$15,000+
- Ongoing advertising and promotions
  $300–$5,000+/month
- Branded merchandise (shirts, mugs, tote bags, caps, etc.)
  $200–$3,000
- Website and platform maintenance
  $100–$500/year

You have the power to select from this menu and craft a plan that helps achieve the best outcome and fits your budget. Most importantly, your investment in your book should align with your style and mission.

Book-branded merchandise can turn friends, family members, and fans into walking billboards who are promoting your book in a single blink. How? With hoodies, hats, bumper stickers, and tote bags—all emblazoned with your book cover and a message about it.

Before you invest in merchandise, conduct market research to learn what your readers prefer—such as a T-shirt that shows your book cover on the front versus a coffee mug that's available for sale at your "author talk" and book signing at the local coffee shop. You can sell merchandise at in-person events as well as on your website and social media pages. Have fun creating promotional merchandise that is relevant to your book.

How to Earn a Good ROI—Return on Investment— for Your Book

Writing a book can be a passion project. However, when you have a smart strategy rooted in the financial realities of this endeavor, you *can* earn back what you've spent *and* profit.

Start by calculating what you've spent—dollars, hours, effort—to create your book. Set the intention to earn back at least double that. You need a strategy that includes:

- Book sales.
- In-person events.
- Book launch parties.
- Speaking engagements + appearances with book signings.
- Bulk sales to schools, colleges, universities, organizations, libraries, events.
- Paid speaking engagements.
- A documentary or movie deal.
- Interviews in the traditional media and on podcasts.
- Online courses + membership communities.
- Book clubs.
- Merchandise.

Now's the time to think like a visionary! Decide which course of action is best for you, then create a strategy to monetize your book. You can use AI such as ChatGPT to create a detailed plan that's customized for you and your book. Here's a sample prompt that you can tweak to fit your needs, then copy and paste it into ChatGPT:

Long-Term Book Monetization Strategy Prompt
I have written (or am writing) a book about [insert your topic].

The deeper mission of my book is [insert your Why and your Intention from your Summary Sentence].

My ideal reader is [describe your Target Audience from your Summary Sentence].

Please create a long-term monetization and visibility strategy that shows me how to turn my book into a multi-year platform that includes speaking opportunities, workshops, retreats, online programs, media exposure, partnerships, and recurring income ideas that align with my message and values.

I would like this strategy organized into short-term (0–6 months), mid-term (6–18 months), and long-term (2–5 years) opportunities.

Hit "return" on your keyboard, then watch ChatGPT create your strategy in seconds. Review it to make sure that it aligns with your vision and abilities. If you want changes, ask ChatGPT to "revise" and describe the changes you want. Continue this revision process until you're pleased with your long-term book monetization strategy. Then the real work begins; you have to take action on the plan to generate the profits you're seeking. When you become just as obsessed with the financial success of your book, and invest the effort into this strategy, then you *will* earn an impressive ROI.

SECTION 8

GET HELP TO WRITE YOUR BOOK

Do you believe that you lack the time, talent, and/or desire to write your book? Don't worry. Help is available! Two great options include working with a book coach and hiring a ghostwriter. When you team up with the best person whose workstyle matches your personality and goals, then the creative synergy of your ideas, their expertise, and the third energy created by your collaboration will feel absolutely **magical**. So don't be afraid to ask for help. That could very well be the solution to finally writing and publishing your blockbuster book.

GETTING HELP TO WRITE YOUR BOOK

Many of our authors sit down and write amazing books without help. Our mother, for example, didn't want to hear any of our writing tips. She just started typing and her life story poured out as if she were having a long conversation with her readers.

Meanwhile, some of our authors work with book coaches and developmental editors. Others hire us to ghostwrite their books.

Now that you have a robust understanding of the process, consider whether you want and/or need help to write your book. That could mean hiring a book coach to help you focus your topic and create a strategy to write and publish. That could also mean entrusting the work to a professional writer who can ghostwrite the book for you. The following information can help you decide if you'd like to seek help to compose your memoir, novel, business book, or other type of book.

Do You Need a Book Coach?

A **book writing coach** is a professional who guides you as an author through the process of planning, writing, and completing your book with structure, accountability, and feedback. This guidance can include how to publish and promote your book.

Imagine: you Zoom into a video call with Elizabeth, and your mind is full of book ideas that have been bubbling in your thoughts for decades. But you've been totally baffled about where or how to start writing from that frustrating jumble of stories and memories that are clouded by fear, confusion, and doubt.

Then you and Elizabeth start talking, and the creative synergy bursts through your screen like lightning bolts, transporting you into a whole new mindset and understanding of your book and its mission in the world.

Next, you and Elizabeth complete the Summary Sentence worksheet together. After that, she helps you outline your book.

And your eyes *sparkle* with revelation.

Confidence surges through you. You smile. You may even cry.

Because you finally have clarity on how to write your book, what to include, what to exclude, and how to commit the time and resources to writing, publishing, and promoting your memoir, business book, novel, self-help book, poetry collection, or other type of book.

Yessssss!

This is the *best* moment!

Elizabeth has guided many aspiring authors across America to this exciting turning point during private book coaching sessions, as well as in her 6 Months to Bestselling Book Success program. You can learn more about it at: https://twosisterswriting.com/writing-coach-services/ and with this QR code:

Book Coaching Info

You can also book a free discovery call to learn if you believe that book coaching is the best option for you to write and publish your book.

In 2025, Elizabeth coached talented Detroit entrepreneur Briana Cobb to write *Through the Concrete: A Memoir of Breaking Cycles, Reclaiming Faith, and Becoming Whole*. During private coaching sessions twice each month, Briana received guidance to express the trauma, healing, and empowerment that she had experienced and now shares with readers to help them create a powerful life. Elizabeth's high-energy, interactive coaching program also taught Briana how to publish her book on IngramSpark. Here's what Briana says about her experience:

"Working with Elizabeth Ann Atkins through the 6 Months to Best-Selling Book Success Program was absolutely transformational for me as a writer and as a woman with a story to share. Elizabeth provided structure, accountability, and so much encouragement throughout the process. Her expertise helped me refine my voice, shape my narrative, and gain the confidence I needed to complete my manuscript.

This program didn't just teach me how to write a book—it taught me how to step fully into my role as an author and own my story with pride. The personal guidance, industry insights, and genuine support from Elizabeth made all the difference.

Thanks to Two Sisters Writing and Publishing, I now have a book I am proud to share with the world and the tools to continue building my legacy. I am forever grateful for Elizabeth's wisdom, patience, and unwavering belief in me."

Briana is proof that book coaching works.

Elizabeth is also a coach with The Detroit Writing Room, founded in 2019 by Stephanie Steinberg, and has helped many aspiring authors get clarity and motivation to write great books.

So, do you need a book coach? If yes, Elizabeth would love to help. Or if you work with someone else, make sure you really vibe with them. They should look and sound genuinely *excited* and energized about what they're teaching and how they can help you achieve this huge goal of writing and publishing a book. Book a discovery call on Zoom or in person so you can assess your compatibility.

Here's a free bonus: you can watch or listen to *dozens* of podcast episodes exploring everything you need to know to write, publish, and promote your book. For the past several years, Elizabeth and Joanie Lindenmeyer have gone live every Friday at noon Eastern time on the Two Sisters Writing & Publishing YouTube channel to talk about writing, publishing, and promoting books.

Since Joanie wrote her bestselling *Nun Better* memoir during Elizabeth's 6 Months to Best-Selling Book Success program, and became a superstar author of three books, as well as a popular speaker and radio host as a result, she shares her perspective as a student. At the same time, Elizabeth provides expertise as a bestselling author herself as well a book coach, editor, and publisher. You can watch the playlist with this QR code:

Podcast Playlist

The bottom line is that you can stop struggling to write your book and get the help you need to turn your book dreams into published reality. If you're anxious about the cost, watch our podcast episodes about how your investment in your writing journey will pay immeasurable dividends, and how when you embark on your publishing path, the resources *will* be provided. Joanie has a phenomenal story about that as proof.

Wealth coach Kathy Kali, author of *Give, Save, Spend: How to Build Wealth and Change the World*, wrote on the Acknowledgements page of her 2021 book:

"BIG THANKS to Elizabeth Ann Atkins and Catherine Greenspan of Two Sisters Writing & Publishing, whose inspiring and compassionate book coaching was the 'book ends' of this book! You guided me from beginning to end. It would not be possible without you."

Now is the time to stop struggling and start writing. We can help!

Do You Need a Ghostwriter?

A **ghostwriter** is a professional writer who is hired to compose a book for another person who is named as the author.

After writing a bestselling romantic thriller with movie star Billy Dee Williams, Elizabeth received offers to write books for people who lacked the time, skill, and/or desire to write their own business book, novel, or memoir.

Her first ghostwriting project was *Property is Power! Building Wealth in Distressed Neighborhoods* by Detroit real estate mogul Anthony Kellum in 2005.

Elizabeth loves to share her gift of ghostwriting—she prefers to call it "angel writing"—and describes herself as a "literary chameleon" whose special skill is to write from her client's voice, so that the book sounds as if they wrote it.

Master Sergeant Cedric King, author of *The Making Point,* marveled at this (Catherine and Elizabeth ghostwrote this book together). Likewise, many people who read *Clear! Living the Life You Didn't Dream Of* by Herman Williams, MD, said the same.

Every ghostwriting project is different. Dr. Williams had attempted to compose his book himself, but admitted that his writing style was academic and "boring." So, Elizabeth rewrote his content to craft a high-energy, engaging memoir that has led to speaking engagements at Harvard University, the Detroit Medical Center, and many other venues.

In 2006, record company owner Kenneth Tyson, Jr. hired Elizabeth to write *Going Full Circle: From Life to Death to Life*, which chronicles his near-death car accident that left him paralyzed, and how he lived his dream as founder of 2nd Generation Records.

In 2009, Elizabeth ghostwrote a novel for Corky Gillis called *The Death Bond Conspiracy.* This required spending time with Corky to learn about airplanes, financial documents called "death bonds," and the horserace industry in Kentucky. Corky even flew Elizabeth in his airplane as part of their research for this suspenseful story.

Elizabeth's ghostwriting clients have invited her on research trips that included: soaking in natural hot springs in the remote, snow-covered mountains of the Pacific Northwest; walking the beach on Martha's Vineyard; flying in small-engine planes and a private jet; and visiting boarding schools and prominent colleges in New England.

When Elizabeth teamed up with bariatric surgeon Dr. Michael Wood, he invited her into his operating room to witness bariatric surgeries on morbidly obese people. The result was the suspenseful 2019 novel, *The Enemy Within.* The novel aims to serve as a cautionary tale about the rising obesity rate.

In 2011, Elizabeth ghostwrote a book for the Morelli family, who together had lost nearly 800 pounds. *Fat Family, Fit Family: How We Beat Obesity and You Can Too* by Ron, Becky, Mike, and Max Morelli recounted their longtime struggle with obesity and how 430-pound dad Ron and 388-pound son Mike became finalists on the hit NBC TV show, *The Biggest Loser.* The book, which illustrates the family's dramatic transformation, was published by the Plume imprint of Penguin Books.

When Dr. Jeneby hired us to ghostwrite and publish *Confessions of a Plastic Surgeon,* he invited us to witness his transformational talent by watching him perform plastic surgeries in the private operating room at The Plastic and

Cosmetic Center of South Texas, which he owns. It was fascinating! And this up-close look enabled us to write with details that readers, according to their rave reviews, love.

It's a thrilling process to bring an author's vision to life on the pages of a book.

Elizabeth is especially proud of the honor of composing the memoir of former Detroit Mayor Dennis Archer, *Let the Future Begin.* This 2017 book chronicles his inspiring life story and showcases how he laid the foundation to transform Detroit into the comeback city of the millennium. This book, like many of her ghostwriting projects, required Elizabeth to interview dozens of people who helped tell Mayor Archer's story.

Including relevant people and their stories and perspectives in your memoir is very important, because it mitigates the overuse of "I" and "me" and celebrates the many people who guide and propel you along your life's trajectory to the pinnacle of your achievements.

Right now, Elizabeth is ghostwriting three memoirs for highly accomplished entrepreneurs and executives.

So, do you need a ghostwriter?

If you have the desire and ability to write your book yourself, please do that. It's the most authentic way to write a book. However, if you want to invest in having a skilled professional ghostwriter compose your book for you, and you have the resources to make that happen, then go for it.

Make sure your ghostwriter has the ability to write from *your* voice and point of view. One of our clients had worked with a ghostwriter who was composing the book from *the ghostwriter's voice and viewpoint.* No! This process requires the ghostwriter to serve as a channel for *you* as the client. Our opinions, style of speaking, and perspectives are irrelevant. That client fired the ghostwriter, then hired us.

In addition, your ghostwriter should philosophically align with you. If your views clash on politics, religion, and other hot-button topics that are relevant to the book, the project is doomed.

How do you find a ghostwriter? Through word-of-mouth referrals. This is a very intimate experience, as you will be entrusting your life story—and sometimes secrets that don't go to print!—with this person. They need to have the utmost integrity and respect for your privacy. That's why you should request references and talk with their previous clients to ensure that this ghostwriter has the integrity, discretion, and professionalism to have the honor and privilege of writing your book. It really is a sacred experience, and all parties should view it as such. It is your *life*, and your hard-earned wisdom and lessons.

When interviewing ghostwriters, you have the right to request a writing sample. Once, when Elizabeth was asked to ghostwrite for a very prominent person, he requested a writing sample. She complied, he hired her, and they embarked on an amazing win-win working relationship and friendship.

Should You Use AI to Write Your Book?

No. Yes. Maybe.

We say no, because the best writing comes from the heart and soul. That's where your authentic voice speaks to you and guides you to tell your story and/or present your expertise in a book.

So, if you think you can expedite this process by using Artificial Intelligence, you will sell yourself short and deprive your readers of hearing from the most genuine version of *you*.

When we say yes about using AI to write your book, we mean it's fine to use AI to *help* you with the process. That means allowing AI to assist you in focusing your topic and even outlining your book. You decide how much you want to lean on a computer to help you. Chances are, even if AI outlines your book, for example, based on prompts that you provide, you will want to rewrite some or all of it in your own words.

What if you want to compose your entire book with AI? It's true that you *can* create an entire book at lightning speed with AI. This may seem tempting if the idea of spending hours and months—even years—toiling away on your manuscript seems daunting and even impossible. Clearly, an AI-written book would save tremendous time, energy, and effort. And it may very well stock your manuscript with keywords and phrases that trigger the online algorithm and help you reach your target audience. You may even become a bestselling author and elevate your status in your industry as an expert who attracts more customers and profits significantly.

Likewise, if you're writing a novel, composing with AI could help you craft the perfect characters, plot, setting, pacing, and everything that acquisitions editors are seeking in a mainstream novel, western, or romance series.

The bottom line is that this is perfectly do-able, and unless your publisher has rules against it, you can proceed on this route if you'd like. If this is your choice, then the Two Sisters Blueprint really isn't for you, because you won't have to do any of the mental heavy lifting required to focus, outline, and write your book.

This book *is* for you if you're ready to organically express the messages from deep within your heart and soul, to showcase your experiences, and to share your wisdom—in your words. This is true for all of our authors, who affirm in our signed contract that each book is their own original work, personally written by them, and that it was not created by artificial intelligence or any automated content-generation tools.

However, we do believe that AI has its place in writing and publishing books, and it's a game-changer.

Elizabeth uses it every day as her publishing assistant, and it's amazing how previously time-consuming, costly tasks can be completed in a blink. For example, in the past, we paid a publishing assistant to format end notes according to *The Chicago Manual of Style*. This took time for our publishing assistant to complete the assignment. Now we format end notes at no cost and in minutes with AI.

It's fine to use AI to help you do tasks such as: organize your content; fact-check; create checklists; compose a press release; re-arrange and streamline bulleted information; and even clean up punctuation in a scene. This is especially helpful if you're not sure, for example, how to hyphenate certain phrases, or where to place the quotation marks around a question mark. You can also use it to provide instructional steps or summaries that help you present useful information.

So, use AI in ways that *assist* your writing. But don't let it actually write your book.

If your mission is simply to create a book that you can sell and use as a credential, and you don't care about the authenticity of crafting it word by word the old-fashioned way, then AI may be a good choice for you. That's not what we do here at Two Sisters Writing & Publishing®. The best writing pours out of you in your authentic voice, and *that's* what deeply resonates with readers who feel entertained, guided, and inspired by the unique expressions of your human heart and soul.

Congratulations, Author!

Now that you've spent the day with us, it's time to use *The Two Sisters Blueprint* to write, publish, and promote your book.

We are immensely grateful to you for entrusting us to help guide your book-writing journey. And we *know* that you can do it! So please keep the momentum going, finish your book, and share it with people everywhere.

We'd love to hear from you. Please keep in touch! You can email us at TwoSistersWriting.com and even book a free discovery call by phone or Zoom to explore how we can help you achieve your goal of *Turning Your Book Dreams into Published Reality.*

Website

Thank you for inviting us to share our expertise with you!

We wish you happy writing!

Elizabeth Ann Atkins
Catherine M. Greenspan
Co-Founders
Two Sisters Writing & Publishing®

About Two Sisters Writing & Publishing®

Elizabeth Ann Atkins and Catherine M. Greenspan co-founded Two Sisters Writing & Publishing® in February of 2016 with the mission of publishing our own books and to write and publish books for diverse people, many of whom have against-the-odds success stories.

We write and publish memoirs, business books, novels, and poetry collections.

We attended the University of Michigan as English Literature majors, then Catherine obtained a master's degree in Writing from the University of San Francisco and Elizabeth earned a master's degree in Journalism from Columbia University in New York.

Catherine's young adult novels, *The Veronica Series*, features a biracial fourteen-year-old girl navigating the world of race, boys, and identity.

Elizabeth's novels include *Dark Secret, Twilight* (with Billy Dee Williams), *Husbands, Incorporated* (under her pen name, Sasha Maxwell). Her memoir is *God's Answer Is Know: Lessons From a Spiritual Life.* And her new six-part self-help series begins with *The Biss Tribe: Where You Activate Your GoddessPower* and *The Biss Tribe: Where You Activate Your GoddessPleasure.* Book 3, *The Biss Tribe: Where You Activate Your GoddessProsperity*, is coming in 2026.

We are especially proud that we published our mother's book, *The Triumph of Rosemary: a Memoir* by Judge Marylin E. Atkins, which is now a screenplay that will soon be shopped to Hollywood as a feature film.

Please visit TwoSistersWriting.com.

Books Published by
Two Sisters Writing & Publishing®

As of January 2026, we have published sixty-three books and have seven—including this one—in various phases of writing and publishing. This list does not include the two memoirs that we published privately for highly accomplished individuals who wanted books strictly for their friends and family members.

2017
Dark Secret
Elizabeth Ann Atkins

Veronica, I Heard Your Mom's Black
Catherine Greenspan

Veronica Talks to Boys
Catherine Greenspan

Race Home, Veronica
Catherine Greenspan

CLEAR!: Living the Life You Didn't Dream Of
Herman Williams

The Triumph of Rosemary: A Memoir
Judge Marylin E. Atkins

Let the Future Begin
Dennis W. Archer

2018

My Name is Steve Delano Bullock: How I Changed My World and The World Around Me Through Leadership, Caring, and Perseverance
Steve Bullock

Husbands, Incorporated: Our Business is Your Pleasure
Elizabeth Ann Atkins/Sasha Maxwell

Remembering and Forgetting: a spiritual journey
Lin Day

First Annual Anthology: Featuring International Writers
Two Sisters Writing & Publishing

We're Standing By
Al Allen

PowerJournal Workbook #1: A 28-Day Challenge
Elizabeth Ann Atkins and Catherine Greenspan

Legacy of a Lawmaker: Inspired by Faith & Family
Alma G. Stallworth, PhD

Broken Hearts: Like Mother, Like Daughter: A Spiritual Call for Equality in Health Care
Alma G. Stallworth, PhD

A.M. Total Being Fitness: Creating Balance
Anthony Moses

2019

PowerJournal Workbook #2: A 28-Day Challenge for Weight Loss
Elizabeth Ann Atkins and Catherine Greenspan

The Making Point: How to succeed when you're at your breaking point
Cedric King

The Enemy Within
Elizabeth Ann Atkins and Michael Wood, MD

The Energy Within Us: An Illuminating Perspective from Five Trailblazers
Carolyn Green
Joyce Hayes Giles
Rose McKinney-James
Hilda Pinnix-Ragland
Telisa Toliver

God's Answer is Know: Lessons from a Spiritual Life
Elizabeth Ann Atkins

Second Annual Anthology: Featuring International Writers
Two Sisters Writing & Publishing

Lifted: A Journey from Trauma to Triumph
Mike Ritter

Confessions of a Plastic Surgeon: Shocking Stories of Butts, Boobs and Beauty
Thomas Jeneby, MD

2020

Enough to Be Dangerous: One Agent's Life in TV News and Rock & Roll
Mort Meisner

Take the Helm: Navigating Your Way to Financial Freedom
Roland Ghazal

Baby's First Year: A Survival Guide for New & Experienced Parents
Eduardo Sanchez

A Young Man on the Front Line: Lessons of War
Elaine Makas, PhD

2021

Life Along the Applegate Trail: A Tale of Grit and Determination
Linda Lochard

In the Extra Years
Roger Sippl

Getting Started with Jesus: The Process for Spiritual Growth and Maturity
Regina DuBose

Perpetuating Wealth: Secrets to Longevity in Small Business
Regina DuBose

2022

MedikalPreneur: The Official Guidebook for Physicians' Success in Business
Francisco Arredondo, MD

Change of Heart: My Journey of Transplantation, Revelation & Transformation
Kristy Sidlar

The Smell of Lilacs: A Memoir
Michal Smith

A Valiant Battle: A Journey with Schizophrenia
Wendel Miser with James Miser, MD

A Different Drummer: My Life as a Peacetime Soldier
Gerard Teachman

There is Gold in the Golden Years: A Memoir
Mary Jean Teachman

2023

Memoirs of an Eccentric Angel
Judy Bohning

Nun Better: An Amazing Love Story
Joanie Lindenmeyer

New Medicine for a New Millennium: A Memoir Looking Front to Back in Time at a Black Woman's Life in Medicine
Sylvia Mustonen, DO

Markers on the Way to God: God's Grace Transforming Mental Illness
Wendel Miser with James Miser, MD

Diary of a Schizophrenic
Bethany Boik

Die Standing: From Black Panther Revolutionary to Global Diversity Consultant
Elmer Dixon

98 years, 11 months, 19 days
Vernon Devers

I Don't Believe It! We're Good? The New Detroit Lions
Barry Schumer

Contains Recycled Parts: My Triple Organ Transplant Journey and the Science of Gratitude
Aimee Mackovic

2024

Joy Notes: Balancing the Trauma with Triumph
Niobis Queiro

Joyously Free! Stories & Tips for LGBTQ+ People,
Parents and Allies
Elizabeth Ann Atkins and Joanie Lindenmeyer

Memories of My Life: Reflections of a Former Nun
Led by the Spirit
Rosie Robles

The Biss Tribe: Activating Your Goddess Power (Book 1)
Elizabeth Ann Atkins

Meditations of a Healed Mind: Welcoming into God's Grace,
Prayers and Invitations
Wendel Miser with James Miser, MD

The Biss Tribe: Where You Activate Your GoddessPleasure
(Book 2)
Elizabeth Ann Atkins

Healing Religious Hurts: Stories and Tips to Find Love and Peace
Elizabeth Ann Atkins and Joanie Lindenmeyer

2025

Armchair Assessments: Existing as a Lions Fan
Mark McCarthy

Life Minutes: Igniting Joy from the Fire of Heartache
Tara Heaton

Pain Before the Rainbow a biomythographical anthology
Jack Cooper

Ten 2nd Chances: This Doctor Died and Went to Hell, Why?
Robert Treuherz, MD

Notas de Alegria: Equilibrar el trauma con el triunfo
(Spanish language version of Joy Notes)
Niobis Queiro

Beyond That Room
Susie Powell

We Are Alike—A Memoir: How A Doctor Leveraged
her Neuroscience Expertise to Survive and Heal from
Narcissistic Abuse
Carol Beth Nelson, MD

Endnotes

[1] *By the Numbers: Audiobook Statistics We (and Hopefully You) Find Interesting,* updated June 18, 2025, accessed January 29, 2026 *Libro.fm Blog,* accessed [insert date you accessed the page], https://blog.libro.fm/audiobooks-statistics/?utm_source=chatgpt.com. Libro.fm Blog

[2] *By the Numbers: Audiobook Statistics We (and Hopefully You) Find Interesting,* updated June 18, 2025, accessed January 29, 2026 *Libro.fm Blog,* accessed [insert date you accessed the page], https://blog.libro.fm/audiobooks-statistics/?utm_source=chatgpt.com. Libro.fm Blog

www.ingramcontent.com/pod-product-compliance
Lightning Source LLC
Chambersburg PA
CBHW050847150626
46549CB00012B/312